Leonard Rossiter was born in Liverpool, but now lives in London in a house overlooking Brompton Cemetery, with his wife Gillian.

His first stage performance was in 1954 and he has since starred in the West End, at the Old Vic, and on Broadway in a wide range of plays. Apart from his two well-known television series, *The Rise and Fall of Reginald Perrin* and *Rising Damp*, he has featured in some memorable commercials!

The Lowest Form of Wit

LEONARD ROSSITER

with cartoons by
Honeysett

SPHERE BOOKS LIMITED
30–32 Gray's Inn Road, London WC1X 8JL

First published in Great Britain by Michael Joseph Limited
1981 Copyright © 1981 by Leonard Rossiter and Victorama
Limited Illustrations copyright (c) 1981 by Martin Honeysett
Published by Sphere Books Ltd 1983

TRADE
MARK

Set in 10/11 Compugraphic Mallard

Printed and bound in Great Britain by
Cox & Wyman Ltd, Reading

Contents

The First Word

There can't be many of us who haven't been told at some time or other that sarcasm is the lowest form of wit. And there can't be many either who have failed to register that those censuring us are usually our victims.

There's no denying that sarcasm is low, just as tackling from behind, bowling underarm along the ground, hitting below the belt, and biting in the scrum are low. But, unlike all of these, sarcasm often succeeds in bringing us out on top – and to many it's winning that counts. Cynical, you may say, but it's a fact.

'Biting in the scrum' is actually quite an accurate summing up of sarcasm, since, as I found from the dictionary, the word comes from the Greek, meaning 'to tear flesh' and 'gnash with teeth'.

Sarcasm is cruel, there's no denying it. To some it gives the same vindictive pleasure as thumping a rival at school in the back when he's pinned to the floor by half a dozen others. To others, perhaps, it gives the delicious sensation achieved by whacking a squash ball into an opponent's fleshy thigh, and watching the small white mark slowly turn an angry red.

Sarcasm is one of the less attractive features in our make-up, but in the law of the social jungle it's one of our few defences. Most of us shrink from sarcasm in others but never stop to question it in ourselves. If Christian compassion or any sense of guilt trouble us, it's always after we've fired our most acidic dart and seen it strike home.

Although most of us know sarcasm when we feel it or

hear it, actually defining it is a different matter. The trouble lies in the confusion that has grown up over the use of words like 'irony', 'wit', 'satire', 'invective', 'vitriol' and 'obloquy', all of which sound splendid dropped into a conversation and hastily glossed over. But what do they actually mean?

I'm sure that people have written lengthy, academic tomes on the subject. Good luck to them. I'm not in that league and don't want to be. The examples and quotations I've included here are illustrations of sarcastic wit as I've always understood it. They're ones that I've picked up over the years at rehearsals, dinner parties, on trains, in green-rooms – just about anywhere, in fact. If they remind you of ones you've heard yourself, that's just proof that, much as we hate to admit it, sarcasm is one of the commonest, and dare I say it, most entertaining forms of humour.

Sarcasm to me is a sharp, caustic, cutting manner which we adopt either at times of intense frustration or utter contempt. It's the means we most readily use for showing our indignation and the weapon we draw when attack is our only means of defence.

Nevertheless, I can't help relishing some sarcasm, especially an impromptu remark from a figure I admire. So, sarcasm for me is really a more bitter form of irony. Much of it is subtle and the best of it is delivered with cool control and unfailing accuracy. I think it was Dr Laurence Peter who described sarcasm as 'the sour cream of wit', and that's the way I like to think of it.

The Art of Sarcasm

There's a story about an actor who went backstage to see a friend of his after watching his appalling performance as Captain Brazen in *The Recruiting Officer*. He hadn't seen him acting for some time and was horrified by his deterioration. The actor in question was cleaning himself up after the show when his colleague burst in. Sensing his friend's dislike of his performance, he pre-empted him by asking:

'What? Bit hammy do you reckon?'

'Hammy?' said the friend. 'You should have been wearing mustard not make-up.'

There's another story about Sir Seymour Hicks going backstage to a friend's dressing-room after watching an equally dreadful performance of his. Hicks went in and poured himself a drink saying:

'My dear follow – it's been a unique experience. I've never seen anything like it!'

Now, to my way of thinking, the first example shows a distinct lack of art in the use of sarcasm, while the other is a masterpiece of mordant wit. And, in this chapter, art is the name of the game.

Art, in the case of sarcasm, is the skill of deflation. Or, in a more colourful turn of phrase, it's the ready ability to prick an inflated ego with a thrust of rapier-like wit.

It's not just inflated egos that can be pricked, though. One of the most satisfying ways of stifling a bore or the gushing idiots who periodically burst into the serenity

of our lives is to deliver a perfectly timed and carefully worded sarcastic snub.

I can't claim to know much about Johnson (Sam, not Ben) but the little I do know portrays a rare brand of crusty wit. Johnson was wonderful with fools. Oh, for his skill!

It's not that I can't tolerate fools. I can, providing that I don't have to put up with them for *too* long, but if you find yourself sitting next to someone who continues to call you 'Mr Perrin, sorry I mean Rigsby', and then falls about laughing at this wonderful turn of phrase, there's not much you can do except shut him up or leave. I usually leave. Johnson would stay, make a remark, and the fool would leave.

Once Johnson was enjoying a meal with friends, but his pleasure gradually deteriorated as one of the company persisted in bursting into loud laughter and making an ostentatious show of appreciation at everything that he said. This quickly wore down the doctor's patience until he was compelled to ask after one outburst:

'Pray, sir, what is the matter? I hope I've not said anything that you can comprehend.'

Johnson's younger contemporary, the scholar Richard Porson, was, if anything, even more admired in academic circles than Johnson himself. Porson was a master of ancient Greek, an authority whose reputation was respected throughout Europe. However, this did not intimidate a very junior scholar who approached Porson with the idea that they might join forces in a book about Greek tragedy. Porson listened as he outlined his scheme and then gave his assessment with this rebuke:

'Put in all I know and all you don't know and it will be a great work.'

Intellectual snobbery is the least justifiable and most offensive form of snobbery. Few things please me more than seeing stuffy academics cut down to size with a well-turned phrase.

Lilian Baylis, the great driving force behind the Old Vic and Sadler's Wells companies, once attended a dinner at London University, and found herself seated next to an insufferably boring zoologist. Miss Baylis, who was only the second woman outside the university to be awarded an honorary MA by Oxford, grew more and more impatient with her neighbour's obsession with ants. Throughout each course the zoologist explained every aspect of the social and political structure of ant life, in minute detail. As the coffee was being served he wound up his monologue with the punch line:

'And do you know, to cap it all, they have their own army and police force!'

'Indeed,' retorted Miss Baylis, 'but no navy?'

When I first started in the business I knew an actor who fancied himself as a raconteur. He used to regard his talent as a passport to a free meal whenever he was out of work. At first his friends didn't mind him cadging off them, but when it became a regular practice, and, worse still, when he trotted out the same tired old chestnuts meal after meal, it got on their nerves.

At one of these recitals the raconteur was telling one of his longer and less humorous jokes. There were a few pathetic laughs round the table and he was about to start on the next when one of the group said:

'Yes, that's very interesting. I remember, some years ago, I heard a funny version of that.'

I admit that treatment like that's a bit heartless, but most of the time people who drive us to the limit only get what they deserve.

Obsessively self-interested people also strike me as being prime candidates for debunking. Failed suicides presumably fall into that category. In reality there can't be anything worse than being a genuine suicide who can't even do the final deed effectively. But, in America especially, being a suicide is good social business. The American humorist, James Thurber, once confided to a young man who had survived an attempt on his own life:

'If you don't mind me telling you, you ought to go easy on this suicide stuff. First thing you know, you'll ruin your health.'

Dealing with fawning admirers, that's to say those who we would prefer not to be admired by, as opposed to those whose admiration we seek, but seldom get, requires the same harsh treatment. Dorothy Parker was approached by a woman at a New York party who asked:

'Are you Dorothy Parker? I do so admire you!'

'Yes,' said Miss Parker. 'Do you mind?'

The enigmatic T.E. Lawrence side-stepped a British equivalent of Dorothy Parker's bore in Cairo during a conference there after the end of the Great War. This particular woman had a reputation among the British population for 'collecting celebrities'. Lawrence's retiring manner presented her with a challenge that she was eager to meet. They met at a diplomatic party that was taking place during a sudden heat-wave. Seeing that Lawrence was standing by himself, drinking water, in the corner, the lady sailed across the room and hailed him with the confident announcement:

'Ninety-two today, Colonel Lawrence! Imagine it! Ninety-two today!'

'Congratulations, madam, and many happy returns,' said the lord of the desert.

(I've always been amused by Noël Coward's gentle detraction of Lawrence when he was in the services trying to hide himself from the world:

7

'Dear 338171,' he began a letter to him, 'or may I call you 338?')

When the great composer Verdi was on a visit to France, he was stopped in the foyer of a theatre by an over-enthusiastic fan who announced that he wished to write to the composer of *La Forza del Destino*, but didn't know Verdi's address.

'I think "Italy" will be sufficient,' the composer told him.

W.S. Gilbert was at a cocktail party when he was introduced to a woman who started singing his praises and those of 'dear Sir Arthur'.

'How wonderful,' she exclaimed, 'to think of your collaborator composing and composing just like Bach.'

'Sullivan may be composing, madam,' Gilbert replied, 'but Bach is decomposing.'

Actors occasionally suffer this sort of nonsense. Sir Donald Wolfit was told by one lady admirer:

'I do think that you're awfully clever the way you're able to play eight different parts in a week. One wonders why you don't get the lines mixed up and speak bits of *Hamlet* while you're playing *Macbeth*.'

'Madam,' replied Wolfit, 'if you're asked to play golf, you don't arrive with your tennis racket.'

The novelist James Joyce had an encounter with a fan, a woman, who grabbed his hand and asked him fervently:

'May I kiss the hand that wrote *Ulysses*?'

'No,' Joyce told her. 'It did other things too.'

Brigitte Bardot was approached by a regular journalistic Romeo, who had obviously had too much to drink and who ended up by offering very loudly to give her a Swiss kiss. Miss Bardot declined tartly saying that from him she had no doubt at all that a Swiss kiss would merely be a French kiss through which he yodelled.

Groucho Marx was, of course, a past master at verbal put-downs like that. Someone once had the stupidity to ask him if his real name was Groucho:

'No,' he replied, 'it's not my real name. I'm just breaking it in for a friend.'

There were often times when Groucho over-stepped the mark, even in my reckoning. A genial priest met him once and spent a couple of minutes praising his films, ending with the comment:

'So, I want to thank you, Mr Marx, for all the enjoyment you've given the world.'

'Thank you,' said Groucho. 'And I want to thank you for all the enjoyment you've taken out of the world.'

Perhaps a little uncalled for!

Tyrone Guthrie had a great reputation for giving the gentle rebuke to people young in the business. During a dress rehearsal of *The Three Estates* at the Edinburgh Festival, he was inspecting a crowd before they started the show, to make sure that none of them was wearing watches, or had dog-ends tucked behind their ears. One young actor, very keen, had gone wild in front of the mirror. Guthrie, walking down the line, caught sight of him:

'Oh,' he said, 'here's a young lad made himself up as a flag.'

The other Guthrie story which connects with *The Three Estates* dates from the first time that the show was staged in Edinburgh. Guthrie was having great difficulty in finding the right theatre for the production. He tramped round Edinburgh looking at one after another, rejecting them all until he eventually came to the Assembly Rooms.

'Yes,' said Guthrie, 'this is it. The moment I walked in I knew it was right – faint odour of sanctity, strong odour of gas.'

The nearest I've ever come to the celebrated sarcastic wit with which some stage people are supposed to be endowed was during my time at the Bistol Old Vic. One of the company, Jimmy Cairncross, was famous for his quick tongue. You always listened carefully to what Jimmy said because he would drop pearls right, left and centre. We were told one day that the well-known actor, Newton Blick, was coming to join the company for the third play of the season to play the lead, to which Jimmy said:

'Splendid! The cast is now as strong as the one in the leading lady's left eye.'

I think that one of the reasons why to outsiders there appears to be verbal cruelty in the theatre is that everything has to be done within a limited amount of time. There is an actual time limit imposed upon everyone – an opening night. Tempers get frayed – hence the remarks.

One of the cruellest things I've ever heard said in a theatre was so dreadful it was almost funny, and it was made by somebody I thought pretty incompetent, a director with whom I worked many years ago. He was giving the cast notes after the dress rehearsal and he came to a very young girl, only in her second or third job.

'And you . . .' he said. 'I don't believe anything you do . . . you come on, you stand there . . . I don't believe anything . . .'

The poor girl was in tears and asked what she should do.

'Go away and be better,' he said.

That famous (some say notorious) Shakespearean actor, Robert Atkins, could make a fairly pithy remark when he put his mind to it. His company at Regent's Park were sitting cross-legged on the grass having a read-through when one young girl failed to come in with a line. She was sitting dejectedly with her head in her lap.

'It's no good looking up your entrance,' said Atkins. 'You've missed it.'

Another story about Atkins took place in a pub just off Shaftesbury Avenue. He was having a drink with a group of friends when an out-of-work, impecunious young actor came in for a half of bitter. He saw Atkins and thought he'd try his luck in case he knew of any work going. However, he couldn't afford to buy Atkins a drink so he watched the group until they'd refilled their glasses and then went up to Atkins and introduced himself.

'Can I buy you a drink, sir?' he asked.

'That's very kind of you, my boy,' Atkins said, 'but as you can see my glass is well filled . . . However, I will accept your kind offer and have one of those cigars.'

Crestfallen, the young actor bought the cigar and left as quickly as he could.

'That was a bit mean,' one of Atkins' friends told him. 'You could see that the boy was broke.'

'I know I could,' said Atkins, 'but it's the best lesson in timing he'll ever get.'

One of the traditions for actors appearing at Stratford-on-Avon is that the leading players are invited to read the lesson at Holy Trinity. However, Robert Atkins, who was, perhaps, not noted as a regular communicant, was not invited by the vicar to read the lesson during his particular season at the Memorial Theatre. He took this very badly indeed and, in fact, spent several days in a bit of a huff about it. All the other leading players in previous years had been asked, and he felt that he wasn't sufficiently

disreputable to be cut like this. One day he was walking down Market Street in Stratford and who should he spy on the other side of the road but the vicar of Holy Trinity. Atkins called over to him:

'Vicar, vicar. So I'm not ****ing respectable enough to read the ****ing lesson, eh?'

Sir Henry Irving had a well-rounded turn of phrase when it came to telling actors what he thought of them. When he was rehearsing his 1882 production of *Romeo and Juliet* there were a number of very eager young actors, cast as the retainers of the Montagues and Capulets, who were keen to make an impression on the great man. So, in the opening scene of the play they set to the thumb-biting and brawling with great determination and violent realism. Irving watched the scene quietly until the entrance of the Prince and his train, when he stopped the fight saying:

'Very good, gentlemen, very good. But don't fidget!'

In 1888 Irving saw Richard Mansfield, the American actor, in the dual-role of Dr Jekyll and Mr Hyde that he made so famous, and afterwards the two of them went out to dinner. Irving didn't say much about the show and left Mansfield to do the talking. When the conversation swung round to Mansfield's own part he complained that the strain of playing both characters was almost unendurable.

'Hmm,' said Irving, 'if it's unendurable, why do it?'

And he left it at that. A year later though, Mansfield played Richard III in his first Shakespearean lead in London. Irving saw this performance too and was even less moved by it than by his portrayal of the Stevenson characters. He went into Mansfield's dressing-room afterwards and found him in a lather of perspiration. Slapping him on the back, Irving said:

'Ah, Dick me boy! I see – hmm – your skin acts well!'

*   *   *

Criticism like this, however, isn't restricted to the stage. After attending a concert in which the pianist Liebling had played, W.S. Gilbert was introduced to the soloist:

'Sir, I have heard Liszt,' Gilbert told Liebling, at which he nodded his head in recognition of a forthcoming compliment. 'And I have heard Paderewski,' Gilbert continued, which made Liebling bow. 'But neither of them,' Gilbert concluded, 'perspired as profusely as you do.'

The English comic actor and co-author of *Diary of a Nobody*, George Grossmith, played many of the leads in the operettas that Gilbert wrote with Sir Arthur Sullivan. However, his relationship with Gilbert wasn't always the most cordial, and there was one famous exchange that took place between them in a rehearsal of *Ioanthe*. Grossmith complained to another member of the cast:

'We've been over this twenty times at least.'

'What's that I hear, Mr Grossmith?' asked Gilbert.

'Oh, I was just saying, Mr Gilbert that I've rehearsed this confounded business until I feel a perfect fool.'

'Well, perhaps we can now talk on equal terms,' said Gilbert.

'I beg your pardon?' said Grossmith.

'I accept your apology,' said Gilbert, looking down at his script once again.

The people who really go to town when it comes to ladling out sarcasm, though, are the dramatic critics. It was Kenneth Tynan who wrote:

'A critic is a man who knows the way but can't drive the car.'

And Edmund Wilson summarised the work of many dramatic critics when he commented:

'You don't so much review a play as draw up a crushing brief against it.'

Some actors, and some shows, particularly a few of those on Broadway in the twenties and thirties when Dorothy Parker and her peers were at their height, have had a real pasting.

She summed up one play in seven words. The title of the play was *The House Beautiful* and her notice read:

'*The House Beautiful* is the play lousy.'

George S. Kaufman attended an opening night of a new comedy on Broadway and wrote afterwards:

'There was laughter at the back of the theatre, leading to the belief that someone was telling jokes back there.'

And Alexander Woollcott gave his assessment of a feeble, sentimental show in a couple of caustic lines:

'In the first act she becomes a lady. In the second act he becomes a lady.'

Sometimes, when critics become sarcastic their remarks end up merely being cheap. One popular newspaper critic had only this to say of a production of *The Shoemaker's Holiday* by Thomas Dekker which was put on at the Mermaid twenty or so years ago. The review began:

'*The Shoemaker's Holiday* is about a load of cobblers.'

The film industry has bred it own brand of terse criticism, with many critics priding themselves on their one-line quips, like these:

After seeing *I am a Camera*, Clare Boothe Luce wrote:

'Me no Leica.'

*　　*　　*

Another critic wrote of the film *Aimez-vous Brahms?*:
'Brahms, *oui*.'

The epic *Ben Hur* was dismissed by one critic in these words:
'Loved Ben, hated Hur.'

And after watching *No Love No Leave* one critic was moved to write:
'No comment.'

Certain critics, however, have established themselves as past masters of the *bon mot*, and their reviews have become cherished examples of tart, trenchant criticism. Of these, James Agee is perhaps the best known and admired. Here are quotations from some of his most memorable notices:

On the British actress, Ida Lupino, in *The Hard Way*:
'Her familiar expression of strained intensity would be less quickly relieved by a merciful death than by Ex-Lax.'

On the film *Tycoon*:
'Several tons of dynamite are set off in this picture – none of it under the right people.'

On *Random Harvest*:
'I would like to recommend this film to those who can stay interested in Ronald Colman's amnesia for two hours and who could with pleasure eat a bowl of Yardley's shaving soap before breakfast.'

On *Star-Spangled Rhythm*:
'A variety show including everyone at Paramount who was not overseas, in hiding or out to lunch.'

*   *   *

On *Pin-Up Girl*:
    'During the making of *Pin-Up Girl* Betty Grable was in an early stage of pregnancy – and everyone else was evidently in a late stage of paresis.'

On *You Were Meant For Me*:
    'That's what you think.'

Quips like these were not, of course, restricted to professional critics. Tallulah Bankhead, the gravel-voiced actress, came out of one supposedly soul-searching, thought-provoking play and remarked:
    'There's less to this than meets the eye.'

Tallulah herself was a good example of the brittle world of Hollywood. She was as aware of her faults as any of her critics. She once referred to herself as being:
    'As pure as the driven slush.'
    But this didn't prevent sharper tongues from taunting her whenever they had a chance.

During one of her Broadway runs Alexander Woollcott sidled up to her and whispered:
    'Don't look now, Tallulah, but your show's slipping.'

Mrs Patrick Campbell said of her:
    'Watching Tallulah on stage is like watching somebody skating on thin ice. Everyone wants to be there when it breaks.'

Fred Keating remarked on one occasion:
    'I've just spent an hour talking to Tallulah for a few minutes.'

And Howard Dietz echoed this with:

'A day away from Tallulah is like a month in the country.'

However, Tallulah was usually able to secure the last laugh – even if it was at her own expense. Towards the end of her career she remarked:
'They used to photograph Shirley Temple through gauze. They should photograph me through linoleum.'

Hollywood itself has come in for a barrage of sarcastic abuse ever since they began to make films there. Moss Hart described it as:
'The most beautiful slave quarters in the world.'

Another critic referred to it as:
'A world's fair that's been up too long.'

Wilson Mizner described it as:
'A sewer with service from the Ritz Carlton.'

And later on as:
'A trip through a sewer in a glass-bottomed boat.'

The mystique of 'stardom' manufactured by Hollywood is, of course, a sitting duck for critics both inside and outside show business. Walter Wagner said:
'This is the only industry that finances its own blackmail.'
And there have been many who've made fortunes in Hollywood who'd agree with him.

Jack Parr put another perspective to the popular Hollywood image when he said:
'To restore a sense of reality, I think Walt Disney should have a Hardluck land.'

Rex Reed expanded this when he said:
'Hollywood is where if you don't have happiness, you

send out for it.'

And more recently Robert Redford remarked:
'If you stay in Beverly Hills too long you become a Mercedes.'

And Robert Evans summed up the glossy exterior hiding the human suffering and sadness in his comment:
'Success means never having to admit that you're unhappy.'

Many stars, like Tallulah Bankhead, are only too aware of the artificial lives they lead. David Bowie summed up his success in *The Man Who Fell To Earth*:
'I'm an instant star, just add water and stir.'

Jane Fonda pointed to the irony of a star's life, saying:
'You spend your life trying to do something they put people in asylums for.'

And Nick Schenk, taking a walk round the MGM studios, observed wryly:
'I've never seen so many miserable people making a hundred thousand dollars a year.'

In the decade after the last war, many of the new stars, particularly the tough, young male leads, were recruited by talent scouts from shops and petrol stations and taken straight from the street into the studios. Humphrey Bogart spoke for many of the old-school Hollywood toughs when he commented sardonically:
'Shout "gas" around the studios today, and half the young male stars will come running.'

Walter Winchell had a pretty low opinion of the general run of Hollywood acting, a view which he expressed in the historic comment:

'They shoot too many pictures and not enough actors.'

Much of the blame was naturally laid at the doors of the studio chiefs – the movie moguls who ruled their empires like despots, yet who seemed gifted with the knack of producing box office success after success. By the very nature of their occupation and the cut-throat competition they faced, these men had no short-age of enemies. When the Columbia Studios boss, Harry Cohn, died in 1958 there was a huge crowd at his funeral. Seeing this, Red Skelton remarked:

'It proves what they always say: give the public what they want to see, and they'll come out for it.'

The great directors, too, were men more feared than fearing. David O. Selznick, whose triumphs include *Gone With The Wind*, had a formidable reputation for criticising the smallest error with lengthy memos to his staff. During one intricate operation, one unfortunate employee made a mistake which he knew would not escape Selznick's critical eye, so to get the ordeal over with the man wrote him a note beginning:

'In reply to your memo of tomorrow.'

Otto Preminger invited the Jewish comedian, Mort Sahl, to be his guest at the première of his epic *Exodus*, which tells the story of the birth of modern Israel. Sahl sat placidly through the film for three and half hours, but half an hour before it ended he got up and said to Preminger:

'Otto – let my people go.'

Many of the subjects chosen by Hollywood directors and producers have also come in for criticism. When *The Taming of the Shrew* was filmed for the first time Ivor Brown wrote that it was:

'A play so loutish in its humours and so lacking in

21

appeal to the mind that Hollywood naturally made it first choice when the filming of Shakespeare began.'

However, attempts to produce anything other than the run-of-the-mill Hollywood film usually met with equally damning criticism. John Simon wrote:
'Any attempt in America to make a film a work of art must be hailed. Usually, in the same breath, it must be farewelled.'

And the distinguished French director, Jean Renoir, with an eye to the box office, said sourly:
'It is in the interests of producers to maintain a certain moral standard since, if they don't do this, the immoral films won't sell.'

Returning to the stage, Ken Tynan referred to an actress in one review and commented that it wasn't so much a case of her being a *tour de force* as being 'forced to tour'.

Actors have had to face up to damning criticism and cheap jibes for centuries. But, it's only in the last century that the invective has become a lingua franca of the general public. Remarks that a hundred years ago might have passed unnoticed by the man in the street, make titillating reading in many papers today. Ernest Hemingway once wrote:
'Any picture in which Errol Flynn is the best actor is its own worst enemy.'

Graham Greene once called Fred Astaire:
'The nearest thing we are ever likely to get to a human Mickey Mouse.'

Margaret Kendal called Sarah Bernhardt:
'A great actress from the waist down.'

And Somerset Maugham, watching Spencer Tracy on set during the filming of *Dr Jekyll and Mr Hyde* asked a friend beside him:

'Which is he playing now?'

Inevitably, there are certain figures in theatrical history who feature in every portfolio of theatre stories. Sir Herbert Beerbohm Tree, the distinguished actor-manager of the *belle époque*, is one of them. There are scores of well-known stories about Tree, but this is one of my favourites, which illustrates how even the most composed actor can be thrown by an unexpected barb of wit.

Tree was nothing if not dramatic in his entrances on stage, always contriving to make the greatest impact on an audience when he appeared for the first time. So, on the opening night of his latest play, he flung open a pair of double-doors centre-stage, at the back of the set, and stood there for a moment holding an impressive attitude and looking straight out into the house. He was just about to launch into his first speech when he was pre-empted by a voice from the gods shouting:

'Next station Marble Arch!'

That reminds me of a story about another famous figure of the theatrical past, which has precious little to do with sarcasm but which has always amused me as an example of the importance of imagination to any actor. That great English actor-manager and master of the melodrama, Wilson Barrett, appeared one season on tour in a play, the title of which I've long since forgotten, but which had a plot that was pretty dramatic, concerning a vicious, angry father, who was very cruel to his entire family, particularly his wife. The climax of the play is where this terrible old man is murdered by his youngest son. On the particular night that I have in mind, Barrett came on stage for his final roar (he had a wonderful voice which he used to enormous effect). He was down at the footlights, ranting and raving with his great monologue, when the young man playing the avenging son came on stage, behind him, to plunge a dagger between his father's shoulder blades. When he reached centre-stage, the actor went for his dagger, reached inside his coat and, to his horror, discovered there was no dagger there. He had left it in the wings, on the props table. He was on stage daggerless. Barrett was, of course, oblivious of what was going on behind him. The young actor didn't know what to do. He looked desperately into the wings and turned a paler shade of yellow. Barrett had come to the end of his monologue by now and, realising that something had gone wrong, was improvising for all he was worth down front. Bearing in mind that the only way of ending the play was to kill Barrett, the young actor, in a fit of desperation, rushed up behind Barrett and gave him an enormous boot up the backside. Barrett, clutching his posterior, staggered forward and, as he expired, exclaimed:

'That boot, that boot – 'twas poisoned!'

Not all mishaps come from behind the proscenium arch. Audiences can be a terrible nuisance, as well as terribly demoralising, when they don't pay attention to what's happening on stage.

At one performance given on a winter evening, John Barrymore and the rest of his cast had battle against the assorted coughs and sneezes coming from the audience. In the end, Barrymore lost his temper and tossed a fish into the stalls saying:

'Busy yourselves with that, you damned walruses, while the rest of us proceed with the play.'

It's not just the actors who suffer when an audience starts to get bored or restless. Recently in the West End, Maggie Smith appeared in a marvellous play about Leonard and Virginia Woolf, simply called *Virginia*. One evening, a couple of Americans, sitting in the best seats in the house, seemed to be the only members of the audience not enthralled by the play. It was obvious that they were not enjoying the evening one bit, fidgeting and clearly at a total loss as to what was going on in Bloomsbury in the thirties. It really meant nothing to them at all. Eventually, the English lady sitting behind them could tolerate their distracting behaviour no more. She leaned across and tapped one of them on the shoulder sharply and asked them to shut up because it was clear that they'd come to the wrong theatre under the misapprehension that *Virginia* was the sequel to *Oklahoma*.

Nor is it just the cinema and the theatre where carping criticism reaches these vitriolic heights. The world of music can be, and is, just as cutting in its remarks and asides.

When a young lady gave an audition on her cello to Sir Thomas Beecham he listened in silence while she struggled through a piece which was way beyond her modest ability. Beaming as she put down her bow at the end, she asked him brightly:

'What shall I do next?'

'Get married,' he answered.

Describing New York's famous opera house Beecham remarked:

'The Metropolitan Opera is not a place of entertainment but a place of penance.'

Pierre Boulez, commenting on the music of the seventies, said:

'Pop music is the hamburger of every day.'

The American pianist, Oscar Levant, gave his definition of musicals when he described one as:

'A series of catastrophes ending with a floor show.'

And Howard Dietz damned all composers when he wrote:
'Composers shouldn't think too much – it interferes with their plagiarism.'

Neither do musical critics pull any punches when they want to express their disgust at a performance or a composition. Witness Rex Reed on the score of the film *Goodbye Mr Chips*:
'To insinuate that Leslie Bricusse's plodding score is merely dreadful would be an act of charity.'
Or the critic who reviewed a Jack Benny violin concert in eight words and a full stop:
'Jack Benny played Mendelssohn last night. Mendelssohn lost.'

More recently I was gently amused by two notices: one in this country and the other written by a New York critic. It made me smile when I read in the *Manchester Evening News* the review of a concert given by a string quartet where they were described as playing more like a 'rubber band'.

One of the New York critics went to see Stephen Sondheim's musical *Sweeney Todd* and was evidently disappointed that it didn't contain more memorable tunes. Indeed, he wrote that he'd come out of the theatre whistling the scenery!

I even came across a story attributed to Beethoven, but no doubt applicable to any great composer. It must date from the time before he went deaf since it refers to a performance of a new opera by an eager young composer.
'I like your opera,' Beethoven told the delighted man.

'I think I'll set it to music one day.'

Writers and poets haven't escaped either, as one might expect. Denis Brogan commented on T.S. Eliot:

'Mr T.S. Eliot, in choosing to live in England rather than in St. Louis or Boston, passed judgement not only on the American scene but indeed on his own fitness to adorn it.'

Robert Bridges was asked for his opinion of John Masefield's poetry by an ardent admirer of Masefield.

'Masefield's sonnets,' said Bridges. 'Ah! Yes. Very nice. Pure Shakespeare.'

'Masefield's *Reynard the Fox*? Very nice too. Pure Chaucer.'

'Masefield's *Everlasting Mercy*? Mm. Yes. Pure Masefield.'

Gertrude Stein, the American poetess whose repetitive style of writing was considered 'daringly experimental' by some, and downright 'eccentric' by others, once submitted a manuscript to a publisher and had it returned with this rejection slip:

'I am only one, only one, only one. One one being, one at the same time. Not two, not three, only one. Only one life to live, only sixty minutes in one hour. Only one pair of eyes. Only one brain, only one being. Being only one, having only one pair of eyes, having only one time, having only one life, I cannot read your manuscript three or four times. Not even one time. Only one look, only one look is enough. Hardly one copy would sell here. Hardly one. Hardly one.'

Novelists have come in for their share of censure, too. Mark Twain sent shivers through many Jane Austen fans when he wrote about a library he had visited:

'Jane Austen's books, too, are absent from this library. Just that one omission alone would make a fairly good library out of a library that hadn't a book in it.'

Philip Guedalla found a delightful historical parallel to phrase his derogatory views on the work of Henry James:
'The work of Henry James has always seemed divisible by a simple dynastic arrangement into three reigns: James I, James II and the Old Pretender.'

Horace Walpole commented on the works of Samuel Richardson:
'The works of Richardson . . . are pictures of high life as conceived by a bookseller, and romances as they would be spiritualized by a Methodist preacher.'

James Huneker wrote of the Russian novelist, Fyodor Dostoyevsky:
'Dostoyevsky always repented in haste only to sin again at leisure.'

But of all commentators it is probably Oscar Wilde who had the most polished turn of phrase and devastating attack. Here he is on three contemporary writers:

On Thomas Caine Hall:
'Mr Caine Hall . . . writes at the top of his voice. He is so loud that one cannot hear what he says.'

On Marie Corelli:
'Half the success of Marie Corelli is due to the no doubt unfounded rumour that she is a woman.'

On Marie Corelli again, this time from prison:
'Now don't think I've anything against her moral character, but from the way she writes she ought to be in here.'

On Charles Dickens and the death of Little Nell:

'One would need a heart of stone to read it without laughing.'

Speaking of Dickens, I did chuckle at the practical joke played recently by certain members of the Royal Shakespeare Company, who have had an enormous success with their marathon production of *Nicholas Nickleby*, an adaptation of the Dickens novel. A member of the company, who shall remain anonymous, had special note-paper printed using the old RSC logo but substituting a 'd' for the central 's', thus making it the RDC, and had it printed up as the Royal Dickens Company. A letter was sent out, in Trevor Nunn's name, addressed to all the bigwigs in the arts, from the Minister of the Arts to the Friends of the RSC. This said, in suitably official language, that, in view of the enormous success of the production of *Nicholas Nickleby* and the fact that they had been performing Shakespeare for a couple of hundred years, a fairly drastic policy decision had been made. It had been decided, the letter said, to change the name of the company to the Royal Dickens Company and to start work on this other great and much neglected master of English literature!

This was only a spoof but it does remind me of Laurence Olivier's final argument as to why there could be no possibility of Bacon having written Shakespeare.

'What self-respecting actor,' he asked, 'would be prepared to be a member of the Royal Bacon Company?'

For most of us, however, sarcasm comes in most handy as a form of social irritant, a sort of verbal itching powder to make others feel uncomfortable while we ourselves stay calm and unruffled, enjoying their discomfort.

Gems may be produced, but they have to be in the right place to be appreciated. Oscar Wilde, for example,

scattered them liberally in the sophisticated environment of East Coast America, but in Dodge City his talents would have been wasted. He was once sent an invitation by the good people of Griggsville to come and lecture to them on aesthetics. He replied, suggesting that they start by changing the name of their town.

As the art of fencing developed into a pastime and lost its immediate connection with sword-play and warfare, so sarcasm must have developed as an elegant means of telling someone you loathed to get knotted. But, like fencing, the art rapidly overtook the necessity and the result is that most of us waste hours thinking up cutting rejoinders to use 'the next time that happens'. F.E. Smith once made the shrewd observation on Churchill that:

'Winston's spent the best years of his life working on his impromptu replies.'

Admittedly not all of Churchill's impromptu replies were sarcastic, but it does give an indication of the great store that we set by being able to appear spontaneously witty and often subtly insulting in even the politest company. In the society of drawing-room and dinner-party coteries, most of us have to leave our natural facility for swearing and telling people what we really think about them hanging in the hall with our coats, waiting to get an airing when we step outside the door as we leave. As soon as we enter any social gathering, a different and frequently insecure being takes over. If it's any comfort, most of the great wits of history must have had quaking stomachs the first time they stepped into the ring.

Gordon Jackson tells a story that illustrates this point perfectly. The lovely old actor, Ernest Thesiger, found himself at an incredibly dull party, standing silently by the fire with no one to talk to. In desperation, he turned to the gentleman standing nearest him and said:

'Hello! My name's Ernest. I'm an actor!'

To which the gentleman replied:

'Hello. My name's George. I'm a King.'

Now, I admit that may not be the epitome of biting sarcasm, but it was all that was required to unsettle Ernest and, of course, he hadn't been offensive in any way, just a little too casual.

The great Austrian violinist, Fritz Kreisler, must often have questioned his decision to become an American citizen if he had many encounters like this one with a New York millionaire and his wife. Knowing little of Kreisler and appreciating his art even less, the couple engaged him as a top entertainer to play for their guests one evening after a dinner party. Kreisler, who was not accustomed to engagements like this, demanded a fee of $10,000, which to his amazement was paid in advance without question. So, he had little choice but to appear on the appointed evening at the time specified by the hosts. In view of the nature of the recital Kreisler had decided that he'd better wear 'black tie' instead of evening dress, but his host noticed this when he arrived and took him aside, to tell him quite clearly that he wouldn't be required to mingle with the guests when he had finished playing. Thanking him for this timely warning Kreisler confided:

'Had I known that I was not expected to mix with the guests, I would of course have come for three thousand.'

The art of leaving on a sour note has been cultivated by many great wits. But saving your choicest scorn for the last minute takes nerve and skill. The last thing you want is for the thrust to miscarry and lose its sting. For all you know, you might go through the horrors of being invited again.

Another guest got his own back on an imcompetent hostess when she met him in the hallway with his coat on, trying to slip out of the door unnoticed.

'So early?' she asked him gaily. 'Do you really have to go right now?'

'Oh, no, I don't have to,' he replied. 'It's purely a matter of choice.'

The most amusing clashes occur when both host and guest are jockeying for superiority. Two women were having tea in the large country house that belonged to one of them. They hadn't seen each other for years and they didn't really want to see each other on this occasion, but circumstances forced them to meet again and sparks flew as they sat down to a deliberately frugal tea laid on by the hostess.

'If you'd like anything more substantial than a biscuit, it will be no trouble getting out the Rolls,' she said, handing over a cup of tea.

'Thank you,' said the guest acidly. 'But do you have the butter?'

When it comes to the interplay between guests themselves the competition is even more intense, since there are no artificial distinctions of 'host' or 'guest' to be observed. Dorothy Parker found herself sitting next to a middle-aged woman who was staring fixedly at an embarrassed army officer sitting opposite her. Noticing Dorothy Parker's critical gaze, the woman leaned across to her to explain:

'It's his uniform. I can't help it. I just love soldiers.'

'Yes,' said Mrs Parker, 'you have in every war.'

Many years ago a Chinese ambassador, Dr Wellington Koo, silenced his neighbour at dinner with style worthy of Dorothy Parker. He had been invited to speak after a dinner in the City, a fact which had evidently escaped the notice of the men seated next to him, neither of whom talked to him during the meal, except for exchanging a few pleasantries. The reason for this apparent rudeness was made clear when the wine waiter came round and one of the ambassador's neighbours touched his sleeve and asked in clearly enunciated tones:

'Likee winey?'

Shortly afterwards, the ambassador was asked to give his speech which turned out to be one of the most entertaining and witty that the group of diners had heard for a long time. When he finished, there was great applause during the course of which Dr Koo bent down to whisper to his neighbour:

'Likee speechee?'

Lady Beaconsfield was the wife to whom Disraeli was devoted in spite of her ability to say the most idiotic things. She once stunned a group of friends who were discussing the beauty of Greek nude sculpture with the remark:

'Oh, you ought to see my Dizzy in his bath.'

She also made herself a perfect target for one caustic hostess. The conversation, as not infrequently, was way over her head and all she picked up from it was the name of Dean Swift, who, apparently, was regarded as a great wit.

'Who is this Dean Swift?' she asked her hostess after the ladies had retired from the table. 'Can I ask him to my parties?'

'Hardly so, my dear,' she was told in hushed tones.

'Why not?'

'Well, some years ago he did a thing which effectively prevented him from ever appearing in society again.'

'Good heavens, whatever did he do?' she asked agog.

'He died,' said the hostess.

Peter Ustinov tells the story of attending a wedding where the bride was, to put it mildly, a lady of easy virtue, and the groom was a nice fellow called Hope, recently divorced from his wife. Ustinov tells of the

speech given by an old friend of the groom, who obviously preferred the poor divorced wife, and who declared that this wedding was:

'. . . a perfect example of the triumph of experience over hope.'

Social sarcasm needn't be quite as malicious as this. It can often become a game, in which equally talented players compete against each other. These people can often be good friends, for part of their relationship at least, but this doesn't prevent them from trying to get one up on each other now and again.

Sir James Barrie used to pull Bernard Shaw's leg about being a vegetarian. He and Shaw were once staying in the same house and Barrie saw Shaw being given a concoction of salads, green mayonnaise and oils for lunch, while the rest of the party were eating what Barrie considered more wholesome fare. As Shaw was about to lift the first forkful to his mouth Barrie asked him:

'Tell me, Shaw, have you eaten that, or are you just about to?'

When Dorothy Parker met a friend at a cocktail party they eyed each other up and down before the friend said:

'Don't you think your dress is a little too young for you, dear?'

'Do you think so, dear?' asked Mrs Parker. 'I think yours suits you perfectly, it always has.'

If it's true, however, that the best way to win someone over is to appeal to their vanity, then it must be true also that the best way to have a dig at them is to do the exact opposite.

'Hell hath no vanity like a handsome man,' said Coco Chanel, but handsome or ugly, thin or fat, young or old, none of us likes fun being made of our appearance.

Before William Howard Taft became President of the USA, he was attending a dinner where the other principal guest was the equally corpulent figure of Chauncey Depew.

'I hope, if it's a girl, Mr Taft will name it for his charming wife,' said Depew, eyeing Taft's vast girth.

'If it is a girl, I shall, of course, name it for my lovely helpmate of many years,' said Taft. 'And if it's a boy, I shall claim the father's prerogative and name it Junior. But, if, as I suspect, it is only a bag of wind, I shall name it Chauncey Depew.'

Years later, during the discussion of the Profumo affair in the Commons, a Labour MP used Lord Hailsham's ample figure as an excuse to take a swipe at him.

'From Lord Hailsham we have heard a virtuoso performance in the art of kicking a fallen friend in the guts,' he said. 'When self-indulgence has reduced a man to the shape of Lord Hailsham, sexual continence involves no more than a sense of the ridiculous.'

The obese Lord Castlerosse was out to dinner one evening when the lady sitting next to him, who knew him well, poked his fat tummy and said:

'Rossie, this is a disgrace. If I saw it on a girl I'd say she was pregnant!'

'Madam,' his lordship replied. 'It has been and she is.'

Sir Moses Montefiore, the great Anglo-Jewish philanthropist, was talking to a business associate in the street outside the man's offices when another Jew passed them. Montefiore's companion made a very unflattering remark about the man's pronounced Jewish features before remembering to whom he was talking.

'I do beg your pardon,' he said hastily. 'It was so stupid

of me. Please forgive me. You look angry enough to eat me!

'You may rest assured on that account,' said Montefiore. 'My religion forbids it.'

Mocking the style in which people dress can be one of the sharpest and nastiest means of attack. It's a reflection on their taste, their wealth, their shape and their aspirations, all of which can be shattered or exposed in one sneering slur. There's the old favourite line about the young man meeting his older rival at a party, where they are both trying to gain the attention of the prettiest woman in the room. The older man starts to admire the young man's suit, complimenting him on the colour and the quality of the material. Then, feeling the lapel, he concludes with the remark:

'Yes, that really is a very fine piece of material. Why don't you get it made into a suit?'

Most of us have experienced the terrible humiliation of trying on something a little more daring than our usual, run-of-the -mill, play-it-safe styles, and being delighted by the result, only to have this incipient boost in self-confidence nipped in the bud by the giggling of the shop assistants or other customers as we parade in front of the full-length mirror.

Usually we are too shattered to do anything but dash away into obscurity to nurse our wounded pride, but there is that band of fortunate few who have the presence of mind to hit back. Edna Ferber was one. She enjoyed wearing suits, the ones with trousers. She was wearing her latest of these in New York one day when she met Noël Coward, wearing one very like it:

'You look almost like a man,' said Coward as they greeted each other.

'So do you,' the lady replied.

Irene Vanburgh, the English actress who so charmed London audiences with her portrayal of Sir Arthur

Wing Pinero's heroine, Rose Trelawny, once met the famous American monologuist, Ruth Draper, during one of her many visits to London. Both ladies were elegantly attired for the occasion, but only Miss Vanburgh was wearing full-length gloves. These were of the finest white kid complementing the rest of her attire, and helped to make her an outstanding figure in the glittering assembly. The American actress, who felt understandably eclipsed by this English rose, touched one of her gloves and said caustically:

'Skin of a beast.'

'Why, what do you wear?' retorted Miss Vanburgh.

'Silk, of course,' said Miss Draper imperiously.

'Entrails of a worm,' said Miss Vanburgh, moving away.

There's the story of that great Edwardian actress, Harriet Vernon, who also appeared with great success as a principal boy. Miss Vernon had a penchant for large, somewhat grand, and the unkind would say overblown, picture hats. One day she was walking unaccompanied in Pall Mall, on the way to a tea engagement with a lady rather higher up the social ladder. She was dressed up to the nines, and wearing one of her magnificent creations on her head. Suddenly a policeman had the effrontery to come up and speak to her, an unaccompanied lady in the street. Miss Vernon gave the constable a few sharp words of reproof and continued to her appointment, distinctly annoyed by what had happened. Over tea she told her story to her hostess. Voicing her outrage at being accosted by a constable in the street, she said:

'So I told him, "My good man, do you know who I am?"'

'And who were you?' asked the heartless hostess.

Hair can be a source of terrible embarrassment – either a profusion or a lack of it. There's a wonderful line of Somerset Maugham's:

'Why don't you get a haircut?' he asked. 'You look like a chrysanthemum.'

Artists and actors used to wear their hair longer than usual before it became commonplace, but before the war, long hair was regarded with great suspicion and frequent disdain. The American journalist, sports-writer and wit, Ring Lardner, was approached in a bar one evening by an actor he vaguely knew. The actor made great play with his flowing hair swirling around his head, while he walked across to speak to Lardner at the bar. When he reached him Lardner asked:

'How do you look when I'm sober?'

An elderly Cambridge don used to sport long hair, as part of his cultivated eccentricity. Most people in Cambridge had accepted his appearance but to strangers he still presented a curious, and some said ridiculous, sight. As one of the senior members of his college it was his responsibility to welcome distinguished visitors, which on one occasion included one of the junior members of the Royal Family.

'I suppose I ought to have had my hair cut for this occasion, sir,' he told the visiting Duke, 'but I'm having my portrait painted and the artist told me not to change my appearance during the time of the sittings.'

'There's no need to worry,' the Duke replied. 'I can see the artist is taking a long time.'

Right at the other end of the scale come those who bravely struggle to keep up appearances in spite of being bald in all but name. In later life, Sir Winston Churchill went to a new barber. The barber fussed around him making him comfortable in a chair and providing an ash-tray. Finally he asked how his client would like his hair cut.

'A man of my limited resources cannot presume to

41

have a hair style,' said Churchill. 'Get on and cut it.'

An alternative reply to the same question, when put to George S. Kaufman, was:
   'In silence.'

Both of these are fine examples of the art of sarcasm. They are brief, trenchant, to the point and devastating. They show the minimum of effort and have the maximum effect. They unsettle, silence, rebuke and put down with an admirable combination of economy and style that every one of us would be happy to achieve. But Churchill and Kaufman were not alone in history – as the next chapter shows.

Sarcasm in History

I was dreadful at history. Certainly there were dedicated members of the history staff at the Liverpool Collegiate School who struggled to get me through my School Cert., but despite their efforts, it was hopeless. To be perfectly candid, with the exception of a few dates, a couple of wars whose names appealed to me (one about Jenkins' Ear and the other to do with Opium), formal school history left me cold. 'History is more or less bunk,' wrote Henry Ford. And who am I to disagree with him?

As an actor, though, I've come into contact with history in a rather different way, by actually playing one or two historical figures. But partly because of my lack of interest in history and partly because of an inbuilt conviction that too much research leads to cranky performances, I never dug too deeply into the private lives of any historical characters I've attempted – Voltaire, Hitler, Giordano Bruno, or Richard III. If the author doesn't achieve his aim between pages 1 and 80 no amount of research by the actor will do it.

Bruno was burned at the stake in 1600, thanks to the Inquisition, simply because he exposed the corruption that made his world tick. Richard III was the target of a masterpiece of Tudor propaganda. Little wonder they had a jaundiced view of the world, branded as cynics just because, as Ambrose Bierce explains, their 'faulty vision' saw 'things as they are, not as they ought to be'.

To some, far from being all Merrie England and smiling serfs, history is more like one long, smouldering row punctuated by choice volleys of sarcasm and any

44

number of stinging personal jibes, motivated by desperation, disillusionment or downright disdain.

Starting right at the top, with God's anointed, kings, queens and their royal relations have usually been in the thick of whichever row has been brewing. That is until this century when they've been reduced to fodder for the gossip columns, though even now the occasional acrid remark slips out.

The Virgin Queen, Elizabeth I, developed a subtle way of preventing her aristocracy from getting the upper hand. She ruined them financially by dropping in now and then to stay for a few weeks and bringing the whole court with her. It's always amused me that these visits were part of her so-called 'royal progresses', though her hosts seldom saw the joke.

Most of them grinned and bore the royal presence, but not all of them took these visits lying down. Sir Nicholas Bacon, who seemingly had a hand in running the Church, got in a good dig when the Queen commented on arrival for her first stay:

'My lord Bacon, what a little house you've gotten.'

'Madam,' her host replied, 'my house is well, but it is your Highness that have made me too great for my house.'

The Queen's jester, Pace, took such great liberties at court that, after one display in which he mocked the Queen openly in front of a crowded assembly and several ambassadors, he was banned from the royal presence. However, the Queen was finally persuaded to allow him back and on his return said to him light-heartedly:

'Come now, Pace, let us hear no more of our faults.'

'No indeed, Madam,' replied the jester, 'for indeed I never talk of what is discussed by all the world.'

It strikes me that a certain elegance of phrase has gone out of the language since then. Even relatively humble

YOU PLACE YOURSELF AT
GREAT RISK, MY LORD,
PRETENDING TO BE OUT IS
A TREASONABLE OFFENCE.

figures at court in the past seemed to possess the knack of being stylishly insulting. Tom Killigrew, who must be thanked for bringing women on to the stage, among other things, scored a notable success over no less a figure than Louis XIV of France, the Sun King, during one of his visits to Paris. Killigrew held the post of Master of the Revels for Charles II, which did not exactly put him into the league of head of the Foreign Office, but even so he helped to sour the *entente cordiale* at a time when Anglo-French relations were virtually at rock bottom.

During their uneasy audience Louis was showing Killigrew some of the paintings in his collection. Knowing the deep hatred of Catholics in England at the time he paid special attention to a group of three, which consisted of two portraits on either side of a crucifixion.

'That on the right is the Pope,' said the King, adding with evident satisfaction, 'and that on the left is myself.'

'I humbly thank your Majesty for the information,' said Killigrew, 'for though I often heard that our Lord was crucified between two thieves, I never knew who they were until now.'

Apart from the obvious pleasures in collecting this unofficial history, it's opened my eyes to famous literary and historical figures as real people. Jonathan Swift, a man whom I had been brought up to admire as a great satirist, had a stinging wit as well, and was no respecter of Dutch royalty.

William and Mary clearly felt a bit self-conscious about stepping on to the English throne straight from Holland with little more than an invitation from a hand-ful of influential politicians. To smooth things over William took a motto, which translated meant, 'I did not steal but I received.' Swift obviously didn't think much of this and remarked:

'The receiver's as bad as the thief.'

It is reassuring to find that royal families and their courtiers had the same rows and jealousies as lesser mortals.
Life at court must have been hell. As La Bruyère put it:

'Life at court does not satisfy a man, but it keeps him
from being satisfied with anything else.'

George II's brother, the Duke of Cumberland, shared his
brother's knack of laying himself open to attack. He once
fell easy prey to the great Cornish wit and playwright,
Samuel Foote, who had already established a reputation
as a superb mimic of leading national figures. He was so
taken by Foote's company on one occasion that he
unwisely said to him:

'Mr Foote, I swallow all the good things you say.'

'Do you?' said Foote. 'Then your Royal Highness has an
excellent digestion, for you never bring any of them up
again.'

It is perhaps little wonder that the Royal Family was
held in far lower esteem two hundred years ago than it is
today. The Prince Regent, George IV as he later became,
was one of the most intensely disliked. He had the habit of
making rivals of men who were frequently his intellectual superiors. One of them, John Wilkes, a lord mayor of
London and vehement enemy of George III, took such
exception to the Prince of Wales that he once proposed
the loyal toast to the King's health when the Prince was
present. This astonished everyone present, including
the King's son, who asked how long Wilkes had shown
such an interest in his father's well-being. To which
Wilkes replied:

'Since I had the honour of your Royal Highness's
acquaintance.'

Even George III got short shrift when he approached a
new arrival at court and asked him amicably:

'Young man, do you play cards?'

'No, your Majesty,' he answered, 'seeing that I cannot tell the difference between a King and a Knave.'

The Georges seem to have had a rough deal all the way. The last one, George VI, got a quite unexpected snub from a member of the post-war Labour cabinet who was dining with him once in Buckingham Palace. After the meal, the King offered his guests a cigar. But when he came to this particular guest the man declined his offer with the remark:

'Oh, no, thank you, your Majesty. I only smoke on special occasions.'

At the time of Princess Elizabeth's marriage to Lieutenant Philip Mountbatten there was a certain amount of outcry as to the amount of public money that was being spent at a time of rationing and reconstruction after the war. Winston Churchill justified it by saying that we needed 'a flash of colour on the hard road we had to travel'. But one fierce Labour critic of the Royal Family said that to have a lavish royal wedding at such a time of national crisis was tantamount to rearranging the deck-chairs on board the *Titanic*.

(The mention of the *Titanic* reminds me of people who have chosen almost sarcastic house names. I knew somebody who wanted to call his house *Titanic* and told his bank manager so, jokingly, when he went to request an overdraft. He explained that he'd chosen the name because of the rising damp. The bank manager retorted, while declining to give him the overdraft to deal with the rising damp, that he thought it would be more appropriate to call the house the *Marie Celeste*, since the occupants were unlikely to be there when the bailiffs called.)

*   *   *

I reckon that in many ways being a member of the Royal Family must be one of the most demanding jobs imaginable. The ordinary man in the street can shout his mouth off without anyone giving a blind bit of notice, but let 'one of the royals' pass a caustic comment and it's front page news the next day. After having a taste of the type of babbling idiots they must encounter every day, it amazes me that they don't let rip more often.

One of the most impressive put-downs I ever came across from a royal mouth was made, apparently, by Prince Philip.

He'd arrived by plane to attend a civic reception and open a sports centre or prison somewhere in the Midlands. When he came down the steps he was greeted by the leader of the local council, an unassuming and no doubt well-meaning man, who was suddenly overcome by the royal presence. Totally at a loss what to say he asked feebly what the flight had been like.

'Have you ever flown in a plane?' the Duke asked him.

'Oh, yes, your Royal Highness, many times.'

'Well,' said the Duke, 'it was just like that.'

Since royalty has largely dropped out of the political limelight their place has been filled in public skirmishes of sarcasm by politicians. In the past, of course, there were many noted wits who went into politics. Sheridan, Labouchère, Disraeli and Wilkes, for example, but most of them, mercifully, had some other occupation outside the political forum to temper their dogma with some reality. It strikes me that most people who get tied up with politics these days can't or don't have to do anything but be politicians. It's a great pity that none of them is a leading novelist or playwright. A Graham Greene or a Tom Stoppard on the back benches might almost make *Yesterday in Parliament* worth listening to on the way to work. And I don't

APPARENTLY, DURING THE
STORM LAST NIGHT THERE
WAS ONE HAILSTONE THE
SIZE OF AN ICEBERG.

think that it's any coincidence that there's been a marked falling off in political wit this century, certainly in the last twenty years.

I suspect that I'd have had a lot more time for politicians if a few of them were just a little more daring in what they said and a little more skilful in the way they said it. I listen to what goes on in Parliament from time to time, usually when I'm stuck in a traffic jam and want to reassure myself that there is something even more futile and frustrating that people endure day after day. But it horrifies me to hear the inanities that are greeted with hoots of laughter. Mind you, it's probably thanks to the general awfulness of parliamentary exchanges that the few genuine shafts of wit cut through and make a real impact. The sad fact of the matter is that there were so many more of them in the past, or so it seems.

Benjamin Disraeli has always appealed to me as a man of politics, a statesman of the old school, trenchant, stylish and supremely effective. Next to him our present lot pales into insignificance. How many of them, I wonder, could write a succession of brilliant best-sellers, get hold of half the Suez Canal, make a treaty in Berlin which stopped a war, keep the Russians at bay, and win the admiration of Bismarck? (A bit difficult to win the admiration of Bismarck now, admittedly, but you take my point.)

His political adversaries met their match in him. Asked his opinion of Lord John Russell, Disraeli observed:

'If a traveller were informed that such a man was the leader of the House of Commons, he might begin to comprehend how the Egyptians worshipped an ant.'

Rochdale, in my native Lancashire, has produced some notable figures: Gracie Fields, Liberal MP Cyril Smith, and an earlier liberal, John Bright. (In Cyril Smith's case 'noticeable' is perhaps nearer the mark.) Bright was one of those northern success stories that got up Disraeli's nose. Son of a cotton-spinner, he not only had the effrontery to make his way in the world with great success, but he also turned into a highly effective orator. One of his admirers, in Disraeli's own party, was extolling his virtues to the Prime Minister and concluded by muttering the old platitude that Bright was a totally self-made man.

'I know he is,' answered Disraeli, 'and you can see that he adores his creator.'

He wasn't without enemies, however. Lord Salisbury said of him:

'He has none of the aversion which men of more logical temper feel for incoherence, even in minor matters.'

The only figure in twentieth-century British politics to come anywhere near Disraeli must be Churchill. It wasn't just his wartime oratory that won us over, grateful as we were for it, but he seemed to possess the important knack of being able to step outside politics and take an amused glance at it, even at times of greatest stress.

In the early stages of the war, when Britain stood alone and the tide of victory followed the Axis forces exclusively, Churchill was still able to joke:

'If Hitler invaded Hell I would make at least a favourable reference to the Devil in the House of Commons.'

Relations with Allies could be tense at times. The Free French forces under de Gaulle once led an exasperated Churchill to comment:

'I sometimes think that the heaviest cross I have to bear is the Cross of Lorraine.'

(A view of de Gaulle which was born out by a member of the Belgian parliament who told him after the war:

'You could have been the first president of Europe, but you chose to be the last minister of Louis XIV.')

When he was told eagerly by one of his chiefs of staff that the Russians must be given the kiss of friendship, Churchill dampened the man's enthusiasm saying:
'Yes, of course, but not on both cheeks.'

In the early stages of the war, when British troops were sent to fight in the Aegean, Hitler made great play of British intervention, which drew a typically Churchillian response:
'Hitler has told us that it was a crime in such circumstances on our part to go to the aid of the Greeks. I do not wish to enter into an argument with experts.'

However, peace-time politics didn't appear to lessen his scorn or blunt his ironic aim. On the floor of the House of Commons and in the political circles in which he moved no one was spared his tongue if he felt inclined to use it. Asked once about a speech in favour of the ill-fated policy of appeasement, Churchill said that he thought that it was very good.
'It must have been good,' he continued, 'for, so far as I know, it contained every platitude known to the human race, with the possible exception of "Prepare to meet thy God" and "Please adjust your dress before leaving".'

Personal jibes were part and parcel of Churchill's oratory. He said of Stanley Baldwin:
'He occasionally stumbled over the truth, but hastily picked himself up and hurried on as if nothing had happened.'

And he summed up his opinion of John Foster Dulles, the US Secretary of State, with the remark:

'He is the only case I know of a bull who carries his china shop with him.'

Even members of his own party, like Neville Chamberlain, didn't escape Churchill's censure. Looking back on Chamberlain's disastrous foreign policy he commented:

'He looked at foreign affairs through the wrong end of a municipal drainpipe' – an observation which sounds like Lloyd George's assessment of the Man of Munich:

'He might make an adequate Lord Mayor of Birmingham – in a lean year.'

Lloyd George was himself a vicious opponent and a master of sarcastic deflation, especially when he felt hard done by. In 1920 he made Sir Herbert Samuel High Commissioner for Palestine, which may not have been the wisest move in view of his Jewish ancestry. After five years in the job, however, Samuel returned to Westminster and, far from showing due gratitude to Lloyd George, only seemed to attack him in the House. Understandably Lloyd George resented this and finally spoke out:

'The right honourable gentleman has suggested that I have some personal animus against him,' he began. 'Nothing could be further from the truth. I gave him his first, his greatest, his most distinguished, his most appropriate promotion. I made him the first Procurator of Judea since Pontius Pilate.'

Before getting control of Palestine, though, Lloyd George had some tense negotiations with the French and with Clemenceau in particular. Clemenceau started complaining about the way that the desert campaign had been carried out and how the Turkish empire was going to be carved up, but Lloyd George turned on him and exclaimed:

'What have you French ever done in the war against

the Turks, whom we have beaten single-handed, except to attach half a battalion of niggers to Allenby to see that he didn't make off with the Holy Sepulchre?'

Another British politician tied up with Palestine was Lord Balfour, the author of the Balfour Declaration of 1917 which virtually set the seal on the Middle Eastern crisis for the next sixty odd years. He was snubbed by Clemenceau when the two of them met at a garden party at Versailles. They both arrived at the same time and went in together. Balfour, who was wearing a top hat, noticed that Clemenceau had turned up in a bowler.

'They told me that top hats would be worn,' he said.
'They told me also,' replied Clemenceau.

Clemenceau didn't have a very high opinion of his American allies either. In fact he was distinctly scornful of America in general:

'America,' he once remarked, 'is the only nation in history which miraculously has gone directly from barbarism to degeneration without the usual interval of civilization.'

But then, as one commentator, John M. Keynes, observed:

'He had one illusion – France: and one disillusion – mankind.'

I have only made two brief visits to America, so I can't claim to be an authority on the nation, but here there seems to have been a marked falling-off of political wit in recent years. And from what political commentators have said about American presidents during this century it appears that none of them has really been up to much. One Republican senator from New York is credited with this observation:

'Roosevelt proved that a man could be President for

life; Truman proved that anybody could be President; and Eisenhower proved you don't need to have a President.'

The one that received the most attention, though, was Calvin Coolidge. For a man who apparently said next to nothing when in office and did virtually nothing either, he attracted a great deal of attention. He commented on his own term in office:
'I think the American people want a solemn ass as President. And I think I'll go along with them'.

H.L. Mencken dismissed him with:
'Nero fiddled, but Coolidge only snored.'

The inimitable Dorothy Parker when told of his death asked:
'How can they tell?'

Coolidge's brusque manner is well illustrated in an account of a brush he had with a gushing female admirer who buttonholed him after a speech he'd made and told him how marvellous she thought he was. This sort of thing is embarrassing at the best of times, but if you're a misanthrope and a misogynist it must be unbearable.
'You were too, too marvellous, Mr President,' the woman told him. 'I'm afraid I arrived late and couldn't get a seat, but I stood up all the way through your speech.'
'So did I, madam,' said Coolidge.

A sentence from the *New York Times* gives an acceptable definition of a politician:
'. . . an animal that can sit on the fence while keeping both ears to the ground.'

One commentator from the pre-war years said much the same about the supporters of different presidents.
'Mr Ford was for Mr Wilson when Mr Wilson was

president,' wrote Hirma Johnson. 'Mr Ford was for Mr Harding when Mr Harding was president. Mr Ford is for Mr Coolidge while Mr Coolidge is president. Mr Ford is a marvellous businessman.'

Political rivalries were just as fierce in America before the war as they are today. Joseph Choate and Chauncey Depew were guests at a political dinner at which they were expected to speak. Depew spoke first and made his usual derogatory remark about Choate. When Choate got to his feet, he referred to this slight, but in so doing turned the tables on Depew:
'Mr Depew says that if you open my mouth and drop in a dinner, up will come a speech,' he began, 'but I warn you, if you open your mouths and drop in one of Mr Depew's speeches up will come your dinners.'

Theodore Roosevelt once remarked in a fit of pique against his Supreme Court Judge, Oliver Wendell Holmes:
'I could carve out of a banana a judge with more backbone than that.'

The more recent incumbents of the White House have proved themselves prime targets for political insults. Two remarks will serve to sum up Richard Nixon. The first from Adlai Stevenson:
'He is the kind of politician who would cut down a redwood tree and then mount the stump to make a speech for conservation.'

The second from the Rev. Ralph D. Abernathy was even more bitter:
'He told us he was going to take crime off the streets. He did. He took it to the damn White House.'

Nixon's first Vice President, Spiro Agnew, showed an unexpected turn of wit when he referred to Hubert

Humphrey's election campaign.

'Apparently Mr Humphrey isn't comfortable playing the Lone Ranger after playing Tonto for so long.'

Another surprise came in the wit of Lyndon Johnson who made a couple of amusing comments on Gerald Ford.

'Jerry Ford is a nice guy,' he once admitted, 'but he played too much football with his helmet off.'

He also said:

'Jerry's the only man I ever knew who can't walk and chew gum at the same time.'

One of the most damning condemnations of Ford's term of office came from Bella Abzug who said:

'Richard Nixon self-impeached himself. He gave us Gerald Ford as his revenge.'

Remarks about Jimmy Carter are still ringing in our ears, but the one sounding loudest in mine came from Art Buchwald, who said simply:

'I worship the very quicksand he walks on.'

But Mr Carter wasn't above getting his own back. After one of his brother's humiliating displays, the President commented:

'Billy's doing his share for the economy. He's put the beer industry back on its feet.'

Of all the British politicians in my lifetime, Harold Macmillan is the one I've admired most for his ready wit. He doesn't just make good remarks but he delivers them well, too. He is a great performer.

Asked once for his opinion of Aneurin Bevan, he replied:

'He enjoys prophesying the imminent downfall of the capitalist system and is prepared to play a part, any

part, in its burial, except that of mute.'

His exchanges across the floor of the Commons could be equally acrimonious, even when off the cuff. Subjected to a tirade of abuse and attack towards the end of his premiership, he blandly replied:

'I have never found, in my long experience of politics, that criticism is ever inhibited by ignorance.'

And on another occasion he remarked, 'A Foreign Secretary is forever poised between a cliché and an indiscretion.'

Macmillan's Minister of Defence, Duncan Sandys, was one of the many Tory ministers who came under fire from Harold Wilson over their policies. As minister of one of the most sensitive departments, Sandys got more than his fair share of invective from the Leader of the Opposition. On one project, the Blue Streak missile fiasco, Harold Wilson really let rip:

'We all know why Blue Streak was kept on,' he began, 'although it was an obvious failure. It was to save the Minister of Defence's face. We are, in fact, looking at the most expensive face in history. Helen of Troy's face, it is true, may only have launched a thousand ships, but at least they were operational.'

(Not that Harold Wilson has lost his touch since resigning as leader of the Labour Party. Only this year he referred to Tony Benn as a man who 'immatures with age'.)

Polished as was the comment to Sandys, it sounded very like one made by Aneurin Bevan to the Tory Minister of Education in Churchill's first post-war Conservative cabinet:

'I don't know what the right honourable lady, the Minister of Education is grinning at,' he said. 'I was told by one of my honourable friends this afternoon that this is a face that has sunk a thousand scholarships.'

Bevan was a thorn in Churchill's side throughout the war years and for as long as they opposed each other in the Commons.

'He never spares himself in conversation,' he said of Churchill. 'He gives himself so generously that hardly anyone else is permitted to give anything in his presence.'

Mind you, he was even more scathing in his condemnation of Chamberlain, about whom he made this memorable comment which took a swipe at Churchill at the same time:

'He has the lucidity which is the by-product of a fundamentally sterile mind ... He does not have to struggle like Churchill has, for example, with the crowded pulsations of a fevered imagination. Listening to a speech by Chamberlain is like paying a visit to Woolworths; everything in its place and nothing above sixpence.'

On another occasion he said this of Chamberlain:

'The worst thing I can say about democracy is that it has tolerated the Right Honourable Gentleman for four and a half years.'

Sheridan, one of the greatest political orators and wits, made this remark in reply to the statement that there would be no strife in Ireland where there was no opposition:

'True. Just as there can be no rape where there is no opposition.'

He once told Henry Dundas, the celebrated Scottish politician and minister, in a debate:

'The right honourable gentleman is indebted to his memory for his jests and to his imagination for his facts.'

And he said of another MP:

'The right honourable gentleman has sat on the fence for so long that the iron has entered his heart.'

Shortly before the American Civil War a bitter exchange took place between a couple of senators, one a Jew from Louisiana, the other a descendant of German immigrants who had settled in the north. The northern senator had made an insulting reference to the Jewish senator's ancestry which drew the comment:

'The gentleman will please remember that when his half-civilized ancestors were hunting wild boar in the forests of Silesia, mine were the princes of the earth.'

The man who comes out best from the war which followed was Abraham Lincoln, who seemed to have a healthy disregard for political niceties when it came to getting down to business. Lincoln shared Churchill's problem with generals, or at least with one general in particular, George B. McClellan, whom he eventually dismissed for his complete unwillingness to get on with the war. In the early days of the war Lincoln confided to one of his colleagues:

'He's got the slows, Mr Blair. He is an admirable engineer, but he seems to have a special talent for a stationary engine.'

On one occasion he replied to a dispatch from the General:

'Major-General McClellan,

I have just read your dispatch about sore-tongued and fatigued horses. Will you pardon me for asking what the horses of your army have done since the battle of Antietam that fatigues anything?'

McClellan wasn't the only one of Lincoln's commanders to test the President's patience. At one stage in the war, when the south looked like coming out on top, he was asked the size of the southern army:

'One hundred and twenty thousand men,' he replied, to gasps of amazement. When someone questioned this total, Lincoln assured him that it was correct:

'My generals tell me that we are outnumbered three to one in any encounter, and we have forty thousand in the field,' he said sardonically.

There were a lot of grave doubts drifting about this country at the turn of the century about the conduct of the Boer wars in South Africa. After a statement in the House of Commons by the Secretary of State for War, in which he outlined the number of mules and horses that had been sent to the Cape, the Irish nationalist leader, Timothy Healy, expressed the views of many MPs and members of the public when enquiring about the commanding officers.

'And can the right honourable gentleman tell me how many asses have been sent?'

Some of the troops who fought in South Africa found themselves fighting in the trenches less than twenty years later. I heard a lovely story about an old chap who had seen action even before the Boer War. He'd been hauled up in front of his CO on a charge of going on parade with a dirty rifle. The officer gave him a sarcastic dressing down.

'I must say I am more than a little surprised that such an old soldier, such a very old soldier, should be up on a charge like this. Have you anything to say for yourself? What was the last charge against you?'

'Having a dirty bow and arrow, sir,' was the reply.

* * *

(In connection with the Great War, I came across one of the best pieces of propaganda I'd ever seen, put out by the Germans:

'The British,' it read, 'will fight to the last breath of the last Frenchman.')

One of the most controversial, yet gifted, political figures of the first quarter of this century was Lord Curzon, who became Foreign Secretary in 1919. Curzon had spent a great deal of time travelling in Asia and this, coupled with a unique brand of self-confidence, made him an obvious candidate for the job, quite apart from the fact that he had experience of government while serving as Viceroy of India. During one of his Asian journeys he paid a visit to Japan. Driving in the countryside one day he was horrified to see a group of women bathing naked in a pool near the road. He asked the driver to stop and sat watching for a good minute, unable to believe his eyes. Then he asked his interpreter whether it was not thought indecent in Japan for people to bathe naked so publicly.

'No,' replied the interpreter, 'but it is considered indecent to watch them.'

This naivety and indignation became characteristic of his whole political career. There are many stories about him, some of them perhaps apocryphal, but they do offer an insight into one of the last great Victorian figures to serve in the British parliamentary system.

Curzon was out walking one day with a friend when, in Bond Street, they came across one of the grand silversmith's shops that used to be there. Peering through the window Curzon noticed a napkin ring sitting on a small velvet cushion.

'Tell me, Simpkins, what is that cylindrical, silver object?' he asked.

'Well, Curzon,' said the friend, 'it is a napkin ring.'

'What do you mean, a napkin ring?' Curzon asked.

'Well, Curzon,' his friend started to explain, 'there are people who cannot afford fresh linen at every meal, and consequently at the end of breakfast they will take their napkin and they will fold it once and twice, and then roll it up, then insert this napkin into the napkin ring and they will use the same napkin at luncheon.'

Hearing this, Curzon peered even more closely into the window and said:

'Can there be such poverty?'

Reaching the end of Bond Street, Curzon and his friend were chatting about their work and Curzon was telling his friend how much he would enjoy being Prime Minister. He was then Foreign Secretary, but Bonar Law was on the point of retiring.

'Honestly, Curzon,' said the friend, 'you will never be Prime Minister. You have not the common touch. You don't know the way people live. That episode with the napkin ring proves it. I bet you have never even travelled on a bus.'

'A bus?' said Curzon.

'Yes, an omnibus, that double-decker thing coming towards us. That is a bus.'

'Good Lord. I haven't ever travelled on one, but I am ready to do so,' said Curzon. 'What do we do?'

'Well, we go to this bus-stop here,' explained his friend, 'and you put out your hand and you will see that the bus stops for you. Then you get on and tell the conductor where you're going.'

Curzon thought this was wonderful, so they went to the bus-stop, Curzon put out his hand and the bus duly stopped. They clambered on board and went upstairs, because Curzon was smoking. They sat down and after a minute or two the conductor came up and asked:

'Where to, guv?'

'Thirty-seven Grosvenor Square,' said Curzon, 'and as fast as you can.'

Right to the end of his life, Lord Curzon went on living in a state of great magnificence in his splendid house in Curzon Street. His family had long since left home and he was alone there but for a bevy of servants to look after him. Once a year his accountant, an old friend of the family, would come to lunch to discuss Curzon's finances. After one of these lunches, when they had retired into the drawing-room for port or brandy, the accountant said to Lord Curzon:

'Now look, my lord, I've been going through the accounts and I've been horrified by the enormous retinue of staff you still maintain to look after you, a single man, living alone in a vast house. I really think that we could cut back quite sensibly, without it affecting your life-style too greatly.'

'I don't know what you mean,' said Curzon.

'Well, look here,' said the accountant, 'let's have a look at this page here, the kitchen staff. Down here we have "one pastry cook".'

'Yes,' said Curzon.

'"One pastry cook!"' repeated the accountant, appalled.

'Good God,' said Curzon, 'so it has come to this: a fellow can't even have a biscuit with his port nowadays.'

On a subsequent occasion, the same accountant suggested to Curzon that the vast house with sixty or seventy rooms, in the heart of Mayfair, had become far too big for an elderly man living alone and that he should consider moving to somewhere slightly smaller. He told him that the family solicitors had come across a beautiful mansion in Regent's Park that was perhaps half the size of the house in Curzon Street, but still extremely commodious, and which they all felt would suit his lordship sufficiently. Curzon seemed less than enchanted with the idea, however, and told the accountant that in his lifetime he certainly didn't intend to go and live halfway between London and Bognor! When Curzon died in 1924, a year after resigning from the post of Foreign Secretary, the Fascist leaders on the continent were already beginning to flex their muscles. Criticism of the great dictators and their henchmen was liable to be a risky business in their own countries, but there was no limit to it abroad. Franklin P. Adams, the American columnist, had this to say about Mussolini:

'*Il Duce*, believing as he does in censorship of the press, will probably cut the final three words from the headline: Mussolini Best Man at Marconi's Wedding.'

On one of his visits to see Mussolini in Rome Hitler was accompanied by Hermann Goering, who had not visited the Italian capital before. When they stepped off the train, a huge crowd was waiting to greet them and they had to push their way through the milling throng to reach their official car. Steering his great bulk through the crush of people, Goering rudely jostled a very aristocratic-looking Italian, pushing him out of his way. The man stood his ground and immediately demanded an apology in perfect German.

'I am Hermann Goering,' the Reichsmarshal snapped.

'As an excuse that is inadequate,' said the Italian bowing his head, 'but as an explanation it is ample.'

When the Allies had finally pushed back the Axis troops in North Africa, de Gaulle and some of his advisers paid a visit to Algeria to show that the French were still involved in the war. During their stay, de Gaulle called a sudden meeting in the middle of the day and messages were sent all over the city to find the members of his staff. One of them was enjoying a few hours on the beach and when he got his chief's summons he dashed straight to the meeting still dressed in his shorts and sand-shoes.

'Haven't you forgotten something?' de Gaulle asked, eyeing the man critically.

'What?'

'Your hoop,' he said.

History, of course, has been full of confrontations between politicians and the general public and, in democracies, where in theory everyone is allowed to express his opinion, politicians have had to learn to deal with hecklers as part of their initiation into debating and speaking in Parliament itself. The way that a politician handles a heckler is often taken as a mark of his skill as a speaker and quick thinker, and it's no accident that the best at doing this have often come out as the best orators in formal debates and political scraps.

'I'd sooner vote for the devil than vote for you,' one heckler shouted at John Wilkes while he was campaigning in Middlesex.

'And if your friend is not standing?' Wilkes asked in reply.

A century later, Benjamin Disraeli was parrying interruptions with the same delicate skill and winning voters to his cause at the same time. To one persistently loud heckler who had only one slogan to shout, Disraeli answered:

'A man with your intelligence ought to have a voice to match.'

Lady Astor received more than her fair share of heckling as the, then, rare spectacle of a female MP.

'Say, missus, how many toes has a pig's foot?' one unruly heckler yelled out when she asked if any of her audience wanted to ask questions:

'Take off your boots, man, and count for yourself,' she told him.

President Harding of the USA was speaking at a newsman's dinner attended by the top journalists in the country. Heywood Broun, who was in the audience, wasn't the only one to detect the hand of the ghost-writer in the tired, old clichés and political platitudes. When the President finished there was a ripple of polite, but restrained, applause, which was interrupted by Broun rising to his feet and shouting:
   'Author! Author!'

When a speaker in favour of disarmament was stopped by someone in the audience making the sound of a cockerel, alternating it with cries of 'Chicken', he calmly looked at his watch and replied:
   'What, morning already? I'd never have believed it, but the instincts of the lower animals are infallible.'

Lord George Brown was at an open-air meeting where there was a particularly persistent heckler. Eventually, George Brown turned his beady eyes on him and called out:
   'We should be a double-act.'
   'Yes!' shouted the man in reply.
   'I'll sing *Swannee River*,' George Brown called to him.
   'Yes!' shouted the man again.
   'And you can go jump in it!'

One speaker noticed that a pimply-faced youth followed him to every meeting in his prospective constituency to interrupt him with the same left-wing claptrap. In the end the speaker decided to silence him once and for all. So, when the youth started up again he stopped his speech, looked at him pityingly and said:
   'You know, I don't mind a girly girl and I admire a

manly man, but I do dislike a boily boy.'

The heckler didn't come to any more meetings after that.

'I wouldn't vote for you if you were the Archangel Gabriel,' shouted a lady to one candidate.
'If I were the Archangel Gabriel, madam,' he replied, 'you wouldn't be in my constituency.'

Each century has produced its own crop of great wits. While speaking with reference to their own time they have often come up with pearls of contemptuous scorn that serve as ready examples of sarcasm for future generations. So let's take a look at some of the great wits in the history of human affairs and see how they fared and what we can learn from them.

The Noted Wits

We all have our favourite wits. That is to say, we all harbour a secret desire to be able to deliver sparkling gems of wit with the same panache and sharpness as, say, Shaw or Wilde.

Whether or not our particular favourites ever actually said all the *bon mots* attributed to them, we can never establish. But the importance of them lies in the fact that they are the sort of remark which our special hero or heroine would have made. It's also just as likely that some of the remarks placed in the mouths of their contemporary wits may have originated in the brains of those we champion.

As far as sarcasm is concerned, there is the bitter, caustic sarcasm of self-defence, which, as I mentioned earlier, I can't help admiring, cruel as it may some-times be. But there is also the sarcasm which carries a strain of sense with it, that sarcasm which conforms with Dorothy Parker's definition of wit:

'Wit has truth in it, wisecracking is simply calis-thenics with words.'

So, in my gallery of noted wits I've collected what I regard as the gems of sarcasm from the minds that I've admired. Thomas Carlyle described sarcasm as 'in general, the language of the devil'. As one who's had some dealings with the devil already, I can't say that I agree wholeheartedly. However, I would go as far as saying that most of those in my hall of sarcastic fame might have been border-line cases when they arrived in purgatory.

*   *   *

J.M. Barrie

The author of the ever-popular play *Peter Pan* and of whimsical satires like *What Every Woman Knows* and *Dear Brutus*, Barrie possessed a sense of dry pessimism which ran through all his work and placed him on a par with figures like Bernard Shaw in the eyes of his public.

Speaking of his fellow countrymen he observed:

'There are few more impressive sights in the world than a Scotsman on the make.'

During the first run of *The Twelve-Pound Look* one of the leads fell ill and his understudy had to be called in to play the part. Seizing this opportunity to make the big time the young man sent telegrams to all the leading theatrical managements and every person of influence he knew in the theatre, bearing the message, 'I lead tonight.' To his grave disappointment this enthusiasm generated no response, and he was sitting mournfully in the dressing-room waiting for his call when he was handed a telegram from Barrie. Delighted by the playwright's gesture of encouragement, he tore it open and read the message:

'Thanks for the warning.'

Talking to a flapper at a dinner party, Barrie was attracted by the girl's looks almost as much as he was contemptuous of her stupidity.

'Not all your plays are successes, I suppose, Sir James?' she asked him, after an awkward lull in their conversation.

'No, my dear,' said Barrie, whispering in her ear. 'Some Peter out and some Pan out.'

Barrie didn't have much time for after-dinner politicians, either. He was present at one gathering, during the First World War, when the men were discussing the Kaiser over their port and cigars. The company was divided as to whether the Kaiser was a despicable, war-mongering tyrant, or a fine man of noble principles, but misguided in his beliefs. Barrie listened to the platitudes being bandied from one speaker to another while he sipped at his glass. But after passing the decanter to his neighbour for the second time he made his only contribution to the discussion which ended it there and then.

'The Kaiser's an infernal scoundrel,' he said. 'But that's his only fault.'

George Nathan probably redressed the balance for Barrie's victims when he came up with the marvellous comment on the playwright's work:

'The triumph of sugar over diabetes.'

John Barrymore

One of the most famous matinée idols of the heyday of Hollywood, John Barrymore was the youngest of the great American acting family famous for its temper and majestic independence.

At the height of his fame Barrymore was considered by many critics one of the best English-speaking actors. He was also considered by his thousands of fans to have the best profile in the business. But this didn't prevent one wretched shop assistant in one of Hollywood's smartest stores from failing to recognise him. Barrymore ordered what he wanted and said that he'd call back for it in a couple of days. He was going out of the shop when the man called after him:

'What name shall I put on the ticket, sir?'

Turning slowly, to give the man the famous side view, Barrymore said caustically:

'Barrymore.'

'Which Barrymore is that, please?'

'Ethel,' said the matinée idol as he left.

*　　*　　*

A party was held for the principals after they had completed the filming of *Romeo and Juliet*, in which Barrymore had played Mercutio. However, through misunderstanding, or sheer effrontery, one of the extras, who had played a Capulet retainer, gate-crashed the party. Meeting Barrymore at the bar, the man slapped him on the back saying:

'Hello, Barrymore, old boy! How're you doing?'

'Don't be formal,' said Barrymore coldly. 'Call me kid.'

Barrymore married and divorced four times, which may have given him greater insight into love and marriage than most other men. He once defined love as:

'The delightful interval between meeting a beautiful girl and discovering that she looks like a haddock.'

After completing the filming of *A Bill of Divorcement* in 1932, Katherine Hepburn, who had played the part of Barrymore's daughter, said to him:

'Thank God I don't have to act any more with you!'

'Oh,' said Barrymore, 'I didn't know you ever had, darling.'

As his career gradually tailed off, Barrymore became more eccentric and ill-tempered. When a leading film producer phoned him one day to ask him to lunch, Barrymore told the man:

'I have a previous engagement, which I shall make as soon as you put the phone down.'

In the end, though, Barrymore was his own worst enemy. Fumbling through a performance one night, he eventually dried completely. Improvising to disguise his predicament he went to the prompt corner and asked:

'What's the next line? What's the line?'

The director, who'd been watching Barrymore from

the wings, nearly tearing his hair out, whispered back cruelly:

'What's the play?'

As an old man, he was asked by a young reporter whether he found acting as much fun as he used to.

'Young man,' answered Barrymore, 'I am seventy-five. Nothing is as much fun as it used to be.'

However, the critic George Nathan also got the better of Barrymore when he wrote:

'I always said that I'd like Barrymore's acting till the cows came home. Well, ladies and gentlemen, last night the cows came home.'

Sir Thomas Beecham

Beecham had a candid approach to his art; he didn't suffer fools and was never slow to say exactly what he meant. The few enemies he made would probably have fallen out with him in the end anyway, and none of his real friends deserted him in spite of the vitriol that he poured on them from time to time.

Sir Thomas was once travelling north by train, and was sitting in a No Smoking compartment when the woman opposite him lit a cigarette. Seeing the disgust on his face, the woman said:

'I'm sure you won't mind if I smoke.'

'Not at all,' said Beecham, 'providing that you don't mind if I'm sick.'

'You don't seem to realise who I am,' the woman told him, puffing haughtily. 'I'm one of the directors' wives.'

'Madam,' said Beecham, 'If you were the director's only wife, I should still be sick.'

Interrupting a rehearsal of Die Meistersinger one day, Beecham took the tenor Walther to task over his acting.

'Do you consider yours is a suitable way of making love to Eva?' he asked.

'Well, there are different ways of making love, Sir Thomas,' the man replied.

'Observing your grave, deliberate motions,' Beecham told him, 'I was reminded of that estimable quadruped, the hedgehog.'

'Thank you,' said Beecham to a tuba player who had just made a deep shake while playing a wrong note, 'and now would you pull the chain?'

On one occasion Beecham brilliantly exploited Sir Malcolm Sargent's nickname of 'Flash Harry'. Hearing that Sargent was going to conduct in Tokyo, Beecham remarked that it was only a 'Flash in Japan!'

When members of the Delius Trust were discussing the creation of a university professorship of music, one of them put forward the idea of having a chair of musical criticism. Beecham took up this point and said:

'If there is to be a chair for music critics, I think it had better be an electric chair.'

On Sir John Barbirolli:

'Barbirolli has worked wonders with the Hallé. He has transformed it into the finest chamber orchestra in the country.'

Max Beerbohm
Beerbohm was one of the brightest lights of the gay nineties. Half-brother of the famous actor-manager, Sir Herbert Beerbohm Tree, and precocious author of *The Works of Max Beerbohm*, which he published when he was twenty-four, he was one of the wittiest and cleverest authors writing in the first quarter of this century.

Beerbohm was married to an American and knew John Drew, the American actor, through her. He met Drew in the foyer of a theatre one day, after the actor had shaved his moustache for the part he was currently playing. The two men looked at each other, but Drew didn't appear to know who Beerbohm was.

'Oh, Mr Drew,' said Beerbohm, 'I'm afraid you don't recognise me without your moustache.'

One of Beerbohm's best known maxims 'Most women are not as young as they are painted' was given a practical application on a memorable occasion when he and his wife attended a glittering society party in Mayfair. All the beauty of London was assembled for this magnificent occasion. There were actresses from the stage and film studios, there were mannequins from all the great fashion houses, and there were Beerbohm and his wife. Beerbohm looked around at the many dazzling and glossy exteriors and turned to his wife saying:

'My dear, you are looking so charming tonight that I simply must talk to you.'

Robert Benchley
Robert Benchley was a famous humorist-writer for *Life* and later the *New Yorker*, and a member of the circle of wits that formed the famous Round Table at the Algonquin Hotel in New York.

Benchley lived in a hotel for several years and when he finally left he was careful to tip all the staff, except the doorman, whom he couldn't stand. As he was holding open the taxi door for Benchley for the last time, the man asked:

'Aren't you going to remember me, sir?'

'Certainly,' replied Benchley. 'I'll write you every day.'

Coming out of an exclusive restaurant in New York, Benchley asked the uniformed man on the pavement outside to call him a cab.

'Sir, I am an admiral in the United States Navy,' the man replied haughtily.

'Really?' said Benchley. 'In that case get me a battleship.'

Benchley was having the time of his life at a New York party. He adored parties and he adored attractive women and here there was an abundance of good food and drink and no shortage of the elegant and eloquent to entertain him. However, the late arrival of a couple of matinée idols cramped the critic's style as, one by one, the admiring females left his side to gather around the stars.

'Now that's my idea of real he-men!' one of them said as she left Benchley.

'He-men!' he scoffed. 'I'll bet the hair of their combined chests wouldn't make a wig for a grape.'

On contemporary society:

'Even nowadays a man can't step up and kill a woman without feeling just a bit unchivalrous.'

Sir Winston Churchill

Churchill's wit was famous in both political and public life for sixty years. This was frequently the gruff, dogged wit of a fighter with a certain coarse charm that has always appealed to me.

As a young man Churchill experimented, as many young men do, with growing a moustache. Like many young men he soon decided that his was not an unqualified success. But before he took to his razor again he had a brush with a saucy young woman who brashly told him:

'There are two things I don't like about you, Mr Churchill.'

'Yes, and what are they?' he asked.

'Your politics and your moustache.'

'Madam,' he told her coldly, 'from your appearance

you are hardly likely to come into contact with either.'

In later life Churchill carried on a long-running feud with that prominent woman MP, Bessie Braddock, highlighted in this memorable clash.

'Winston, you're drunk,' Bessie Braddock told Churchill on one occasion when they were seated next to each other at a meal.

'Bessie, you're ugly but tomorrow morning I'll be sober,' Churchill told her.

Bernard Shaw and Churchill were often at loggerheads. The story which sums up their rivalry for me is the one about the theatre tickets: Shaw sent Churchill two tickets for the opening night of one of his plays. Attached to them was a note saying:

'Bring a friend, if you have one.'

Churchill sent back the tickets saying that he wasn't free on that evening but that he would like a couple of tickets . . .

'For the second night, if you have one.'

During his first ministry after the war, Churchill had a very go-ahead Minister of Public Works who was full of new ideas for transforming the war-damaged country into a super-metropolis of the 1950s. Churchill was less enthusiastic about his plans, though, and dampened the man's ardour with the warning:

'Do not let spacious plans for a new world divert your energies from saving what is left of the old.'

The labour MP Herbert Morrison served in Churchill's wartime cabinet as Home Secretary and Minister of Home Security and in that time Churchill came to know his style of ministerial work well. Later, Morrison was in the forefront of the postwar social revolution as Leader of the Commons, deputy Prime Minister and

Lord President of the Council. During one of the many debates on the wave of social legislation that was passed under that Labour government Churchill remarked of one passage in a Bill:

'Here I see the hand of the master craftsman, the Lord President.'

'The right honourable gentleman has promoted me,' said Morrison.

'Craft is common to both skill and deceit,' said Churchill.

Churchill didn't have it all his own way. A.J. Balfour once said of one of his books:

'I am immersed in Winston's brilliant autobiography, disguised as a history of the universe.'

Sir Noël Coward

Although several of my favourite Coward stories appear elsewhere in this book he must rank among the 'Noted Wits' and accordingly deserves inclusion here.

I have a Coward story which I believe is little known and which gives an idea of the Master's wonderful impromptu ability to put people in their place. I was being examined by a doctor in Wimpole Street, and it is to him that I owe this unique confidence. He assured me that this was his own, personal, true story of Coward.

The doctor had been asked to give Coward a medical examination for the insurance on him during the shooting of *Our Man in Havana*. The doctor's patients normally went to his surgery, but in this case the doctor had to go to the Savoy. He examined Coward thoroughly and at the end asked him for a urine sample.

'No, no,' said Coward, 'it's really out of the question, quite impossible.'

'Just a teaspoonful?' asked the doctor.

'I haven't a teaspoon on me,' said Coward, showing him the door.

Coward was being filmed for an interview with the BBC. The sound-man and he just didn't hit it off. The sound-man had a little clip-on microphone that he was determined to attach to Coward's tie which, though extremely bright, not to say garish, was of course of the best quality silk. Every time Coward spoke he moved his head about and the rustling of this exotic tie made it impossible for any of the interview to be heard. When he came to see the interview afterwards he looked at the film and said:

'Ah, yes – just as I thought. My tie was far too loud.'

Somebody rushed into a party and announced that a friend of several of the people present and an acquaintance of all of them – who was, it has to be admitted, a notorious bore – had taken a gun to his head and blown out his brains. Coward quipped:

'He must have been a frightfully good shot.'

Cole Lesley and Noël Coward went into a travel agency to book a holiday to Pago Pago, which is pronounced Pango Pango in spite of the fact that the original spelling was Pango Pango. They were told this interesting piece of orthographic information by the travel agent looking after them, who explained that the reason was that when the maps were printed the compositor ran out of 'n's' by the time he got to this insignificant little island, so he named it Pago Pago instead of Pango Pango.

'Well, well, we live and learn,' said Coward.

'Yes,' said the travel agent. 'Then we die and forget it all.'

Douglas Jerrold
Although he was only fifty-four when he died in 1857, Douglas Jerrold had established himself as one of the

leading early Victorian wits. The son of an actor and entirely self-educated, he became a popular dramatist and humorist, writing for *Punch* and *Lloyd's Weekly Newspaper*, as well as writing novels.

A true wit, Jerrold had a ready turn of phrase which he could bring into play in a flash. Bored to distraction by a very thin man in whose company he found himself Jerrold finally silenced him with the curt observation:

'Sir, you are like a pin, but without either its head or its point.'

Reading *Blackwood's Magazine* one day, Jerrold came across an article by a fellow contributor to *Punch*, Albert Smith. Jerrold, who had little regard for Smith, read the article and, coming to the end, noticed the initials A.S.

'What a pity Smith will only tell two-thirds of the truth,' he said as he tossed the magazine aside.

On the opening night of his melodrama *Fifteen Years of a Drunkard's Life*, Jerrold was understandably a little edgy. (Who wouldn't be with a title like that?) Hovering round the entrance to the theatre he was greeted by a fellow playwright who gave him the comforting reassurance:

'I never feel nervous on the first night of any of my pieces.'

'Well, sir, you have the advantage over me there,' said Jerrold. 'You are always certain of success. Your pieces have all been tried before.'

Jerrold was a drinking man and had severe misgivings about the temperance movement which was gathering momentum towards the end of his life. George Cruikshank, the great caricaturist, was one of the most powerful converts to the movement and his series of drawings called *The Bottle* had a great effect on the drinking public. Such was his zeal for converts that

Jerrold met him campaigning in the street one day and said:

'Now, my dear George, do remember that water is very good everywhere – except on the brain.'

Jerrold had no time either for those who wanted to form a closer alliance with France. During one of his visits to Paris, he was button-holed by an enthusiastic Frenchman who bombarded him with reasons for the establishment of an *entente cordiale* between the two countries. Having exhausted his patience and his wine, Jerrold rose from the table and left, saying:

'The best thing I know between France and England is the sea.'

Jerrold became trapped in conversation with a tedious man seated next to him at dinner, who did nothing but flaunt his intellectual achievements. He even went as far as comparing himself to Peter Abelard, the great medieval scholar, and comparing his wife to Héloise, Abelard's famous mistress. His wife had been brought up in a convent, he explained, and was on the point of taking the veil when they met. His many gifts captivated her heart, and she renounced her calling, choosing to follow him instead.

'Ah! She evidently thought you better than nun,' remarked Jerrold.

Dr Johnson

Johnson had a brand of crusty humour which has become accepted as typical of the wit of the eighteenth century. He said what he felt and he feared no confrontation. He knew he was right and, even when he wasn't, he refused to accept the fact.

Johnson's biographer and lifelong friend, James Boswell, was frequently the subject of the doctor's censure and scorn. On their first meeting Boswell apologised:

'Mr Johnson, I do indeed come from Scotland, but I can't help it.'

Johnson replied:

'That, sir, I find is what a great many of your countrymen cannot help.'

During their tour of Scotland, Boswell pointed to the social advantages the Scots had over the English, observing that there was seldom a case of a beggar dying in the street in Scotland.

'I believe, sir, you are right,' Johnson told him, 'but this does not arise from the want of beggars, but the impossibility of starving a Scotsman.'

When it came to matters of art, Johnson was even less unbending. Boswell once asked him at dinner whether he wouldn't agree that a good cook was more of an asset to a community than a good poet.

'I don't suppose that there's a dog in the town, but what thinks so,' said Johnson sourly.

Asked by a lady what he thought about music and whether he agreed that it was the most satisfying of the arts, Johnson said:

'No, madam, but of all noises, I think music is the least disagreeable.'

In company he refused to adopt the conventional façade of accepted good manners.

'Why, doctor, I believe you prefer the company of men to that of ladies,' one indignant, but very talkative, woman told him, when she noticed his attention had wandered from what she was saying.

'Madam,' Johnson replied, 'I am very fond of the company of ladies. I like their beauty, I like their delicacy, I like their vivacity and I like their silence.'

A combination of his two pet hates – music and ostentatious display – brought a suitably acrid response from him when he found himself forced to listen to his hostess playing her harpsichord one evening. By way of mitigation, she told him when she finished:

'Do you know, doctor, that selection is very difficult?'

'Difficult, madam!' he retorted. 'Would to heaven it had been impossible.'

Bores and fools got short shrift from Johnson. One unfortunate victim, meeting Johnson and Boswell in the street, would have liked to have talked at length with them, but for Johnson's summary dismissal:

'That fellow seems to possess but one idea, and that is the wrong one.'

Talking one day with a man who followed a worthless and demoralising business, Johnson reproved him for squandering his efforts.

'Well, you know, doctor, I have to live,' the man told him.

'I don't see the least necessity for that,' said Johnson, passing on.

When a friend introduced his brother to Johnson he tried to recommend him to the great man's notice by remarking:

'When we have sat together some time, you'll find my brother growing very interesting.'

Johnson thanked him for this advice, but said that he could wait.

Surprisingly, one of the men who supported Johnson's attitude to society and who accepted the need for his peculiar humour, was the Scottish minister and historian, William Robertson. He once defended Johnson's jokes and jibes on the basis that they were the rebukes of the righteous, which the scriptures described as being like an excellent oil.

'Yes, indeed,' said Edmund Burke, to whom he was speaking. 'Oil of vitriol.'

Charles Lamb

Charles Lamb is one of the best-known and best-loved essayists in the English language. A friend of Coleridge and Wordsworth, he struggled throughout his life against poverty, his stutter, and the tragedy of his sister's madness, while losing nothing of the humour or sense of fun which endeared him to his friends and readers. The strain under which he lived lent his wit a mordant quality which many of the stories about him show.

Wordsworth once said to him:

'I believe that I could write like Shakespeare, if I had a mind to try it.'

'Yes,' said Lamb. 'Nothing wanting but the mind.'

Commenting on their long friendship, Coleridge once said to him:

'I believe you never heard me preach, Charles?' referring to the time when he was a Unitarian minister.

'Yes,' Lamb corrected him, 'I believe I never heard you do anything else.'

'What are you about, Mr Lamb?' a superior asked him in the office one day.

'About forty,' replied Lamb.

'I like not your answer,' said the man haughtily.

'Nor I your question,' said Lamb, getting back to his work.

Oscar Levant

Writer, pianist and wit, Oscar Levant had one of the sharpest tongues in America this century. A friend and associate of leading artists and musicians, he was also one of their most outspoken critics.

To the composer, George Gershwin:
'Tell me, George, if you had to do it all over, would you fall in love with yourself again?'

On Leonard Bernstein:
'Leonard Bernstein uses music as an accompaniment to his conducting.'

And:
'I think a lot of Bernstein, but not as much as he does.'

Speaking of actress Doris Day, Levant said:
'I knew her before she was a virgin.'

When Gershwin died there were many tributes to him and one fan even composed an elegy which Levant grudgingly agreed to hear. The composer played his piece on the piano and then asked Levant what he thought of it.
'I think it would have been better if you had died and Gershwin had written the elegy.'

There were remarks on the other side of the coin, though, which gave Levant as good as he gave himself. Alexander Woollcott said:
'There's nothing wrong with Oscar Levant – nothing that a miracle couldn't fix.'

And one commentator in the *New York Times* described him as:
'The lap-dog with rabies.'

Abraham Lincoln
Lincoln never wished to be looked upon as an angel and he certainly never failed to rebuke or put down others

who, in his opinion, got above themselves.

A friend took him to see the latest canvas of a very indifferent artist and asked his opinion of it. Lincoln appeared to study the picture for a moment or two and then said:

'The painter is a very good painter and observes the Lord's commandments.'

'What do you mean by that?' the friend asked.

'Why, I think that he hath not made to himself the likeness of anything that is in heaven above, or that is in the earth beneath or that is in the waters under the earth.'

Shortly after the beginning of the Civil War, Lincoln was talking to a clergyman after a service he'd been attending when the priest commented solemnly:

'Let us have faith, Mr President, that the Lord is on our side in this great struggle.'

'I am not at all concerned about that, for I know that the Lord is always on the side of the right,' said Lincoln, 'but it is my constant anxiety and prayer that I and this nation may be on the Lord's side.'

While championing the cause of the underdog, Lincoln had no time for the imperious or big-headed. A lady of just such bearing approached him once demanding a post in the army for her son.

'Mr President, you must give me a colonel's commission for my son,' she said unequivocally. 'Sir, I demand it, not as a favour, but as a right. Sir, my grandfather fought at Lexington. Sir, my uncle was the only man that did not run away at Bladensburg. Sir, my father fought at New Orleans, and my husband was killed at Monterey.'

'I guess, madam, your family has done enough for the country,' Lincoln told her. 'I think the time has come to give somebody else a chance.'

*   *   *

A Congressman from New Jersey brought two of his fellow citizens from the state to the White House to meet the President. Hoping that he could persuade Lincoln to take notice of them, he introduced them as 'two of the weightiest men in southern New Jersey', and then proceeded to extol their virtues in heavy, ponderous terms. When they eventually left the President's office, Lincoln remarked to one of his aides:

'I wonder that end of the state didn't tip up when they got off it.'

When he was practising at the bar, Lincoln found himself opposite a lawyer who objected to the bench that one of the jury knew Mr Lincoln, which he maintained was a reflection on the honour of a lawyer. The judge over-ruled the objection. When Lincoln discovered that two or three of the jury knew his opponent and reported this fact, the judge said that Lincoln was wasting time.

'The mere fact that a juror knows your opponent does not disqualify him,' said the judge.

'No, your Honour,' Lincoln replied. 'But I am afraid that some of the gentlemen may not know him which would place me at a disadvantage.'

Groucho Marx
Groucho needs no introduction, since his Marxisms are becoming at least as well known (if not better known) as those of the other Marx, Karl.

Speaking at a screenwriters' dinner:
'We in the industry know that behind every successful screenwriter stands a woman. And behind her stands his wife.'

On television.
'I must say I find television very educational. The

97

minute somebody turns it on, I go into the library and read a good book.'

Asked for his opinion of sex, he said:
'I think it's here to stay.'

On a man with a very full beard:
'I've heard of the five o'clock shadow, but this is ridiculous.'

'Oh, I just love Nature,' an obese dowager, festooned with chins and rolls of fat, told Groucho.
'That's loyalty,' he replied, 'after what Nature did to you.'

Four years after the release of *Casablanca*, Warner Brothers threatened to sue the Marx brothers for calling their latest film *A Night in Casablanca*, because they had used the name Casablanca. Groucho replied:
'I'll sue you for using the word *Brothers*.'

To a bellboy paging him in a New York restaurant:
'Will you do me a favour and stop yelling my name all over this restaurant. Do I go round yelling your name?'

'Mistresses are more common in California – in fact, some of them are very common. It's easier for a man to conceal his mistress there because of the smog.'

Dorothy Parker
Dorothy Parker has become idealised as the archetypal wit of the roaring twenties. Whether or not she said half the wisecracks or one-line winners credited to her I have no idea, but from her writings and book reviews she certainly appears to match Alexander Woollcott's description of 'a combination of Little Nell and Lady Macbeth.' She embraced both the main categories of wit, the considered wit of the writer

and the spontaneous wit of the conversationalist, yet she managed to give to both a freshness that swept aside any conscious artifice. Here she is reviewing books for the *New Yorker*.

Describing Margot Asquith's autobiography (four volumes of it) she wrote:
'The affair between Margot Asquith and Margot Asquith will live as one of the prettiest love stories in all literature.'

After the publication of another work by the English lady, *Lay Sermons*, her review read:
'*Lay Sermons* is a naïve and an annoying and an unimportant book. The author says "I am not sure that my ultimate choice for the name of this modest work is altogether happy." Happier I think it would have been if, instead of the word "Sermons", she had selected the word "off".'

Commenting on a book on science she wrote:
'It was written without fear and without research.'

When she was told that a friend had broken her leg while visiting London, Dorothy Parker commented:
'Probably sliding down a barrister.'

When someone told her that a celebrated she-male was visiting the USA to see her mother, Dorothy Parker said:
'And what sex, may I ask, is the mother?'

After reading A.A. Milne's *Winnie the Pooh*, she wrote in her Constant Reader column in the *New Yorker*:
'Tonstant Weader fwowed up.'

On the dancer, Isadora Duncan:
'She ran ahead, where there were no paths.'

*　　*　　*

On show business:
'Scratch an actor and you'll find an actress.'

On herself:
'I was the toast of two continents: Greenland and Australia.'

On the English actor, Basil Rathbone:
'Two profiles pasted together.'

George Bernard Shaw
Shaw gave the English language an adjective coined from his work and style – 'Shavian' – which no other great wit can claim to have done. Brittle and sharp as his humour was, it never lacked point and was seldom gratuitous.

On marriage:
'Marriage is the only legal contract which abrogates as between the parties all the laws that safeguard the particular relation to which it refers.'

On a leading patron of the arts at the turn of the century:
'He's a man of great common sense and good taste ... meaning thereby a man without originality or moral courage.'

Before Gabriel Pascal acquired the film rights for Shaw's plays, many film producers had tried unsuccessfully to persuade Shaw to sell them. One of these was Samuel Goldwyn. Goldwyn apparently found Shaw's terms too much and attempted to bring down his price by appealing to the artist in him:
'Think of the millions of people who would get a chance to see your plays who would otherwise never see them. Think of the contribution it would be to art,'

he told the playwright. But Shaw was unmoved and simply replied:

'The trouble is, Mr Goldwyn, that you think of nothing but art and I think of nothing but money.'

'Self-sacrifice enables us to sacrifice other people without blushing.'

Shaw was rummaging through a pile of books marked 'reduced', in a second-hand bookshop, when he came across a volume of his own plays. Looking inside he saw that it was inscribed to a friend and carried the message 'With the compliments of George Bernard Shaw.' He bought the book for a few pence and added a second inscription – 'With the renewed compliments of George Bernard Shaw', and sent it back to its former owner.

'Democracy substitutes election by the incompetent many for appointment by the corrupt few.'

When Shaw was asked whether he would like his name included in an honours list he replied that only a Dukedom would be sufficient.

'Gambling promises the poor what property performs for the rich: that is why the bishops dare not denounce it fundamentally.'

'Liberty means responsibility. That is why most men dread it.'

'There are no secrets better kept than the secrets that everybody guesses.'

'Except during the nine months before he draws his first breath, no man manages his affairs as well as a tree does.'

*　　*　　*

'The more things a man is ashamed of, the more respectable he is.'

To an actress who sent him a telegram reading 'AM CRAZY TO PLAY SAINT JOAN', Shaw cabled back: 'I QUITE AGREE.'

Shaw was once sent an invitation which informed him that his would-be hostess would be 'at home' at a certain time on a day a fortnight after the date on the envelope. Shaw replied:
   'GBS also.'

F.E. Smith
F.E. Smith, later Lord Birkenhead, had one of the most distinguished (and entertaining) legal careers of this century. A brilliant academic lawyer, Smith entered Parliament and in his provocative maiden speech established a reputation as an equally gifted orator and wit. He was made Lord Chancellor and served as Secretary of State for India for four years. But, from his early days in the courtroom to his time in the House of Lords, he maintained a defiant independence of mind and spontaneity in conversation, even in heated exchange.

He crossed swords with Judge Wills on two notable occasions when he appeared before his bench. In the first, F.E. argued with his lordship for so long that the judge finally interrupted him sternly.
   'Whatever do you think I'm on the bench for, young man?'
   'It is not for me, m'lud, to attempt to fathom the inscrutable workings of Providence,' answered the young lawyer, unabashed.

Many years after taking a BCL at Oxford, Lord Birkenhead found himself refusing silk to the university professor who had only awarded him a second class in his degree, after he had presented himself, as plain F.E. Smith, for the oral part of the exam, the *viva voce*. Not one to lose a chance of getting his own back, even after all that time, Smith explained to the man:

'Silk is only awarded to academic lawyers of distinction.'

When he was created Lord Chancellor, he was congratulated by Horatio Bottomley, who had already been acquitted of fraud and who had no less than sixty-seven bankruptcy petitions and writs filed against him in the space of five years.

'Upon my soul, F.E., I shouldn't have been surprised to hear that you had been made Archbishop of Canterbury,' said Bottomley.

'If I had, I should have asked you to come to my installation,' replied Lord Birkenhead.

'That's damned nice of you,' said Bottomley.

'Not at all. I should have needed a crook.'

F.E. was speaking at the Cambridge Union one night, and was giving one of his most entertaining and memorable speeches, when a small voice at the back of the chamber interrupted him.

'Stand up, sir,' bellowed F.E. Silence fell on the audience as a wretched-looking undergraduate got to his feet. The youth looked about shamefacedly.

'Sit down, sir,' bellowed F.E. eventually. 'The insignificance of your appearance is sufficient to answer to the impudence of your interruption.'

On Austen Chamberlain, Chancellor of the Exchequer and brother of Neville Chamberlain:

'Austen always played the game and always lost.'

Sydney Smith
Sydney Smith was a remarkable late eighteenth-

century and early nineteenth-century author, clergyman and wit. He possessed the power to argue lucidly
and powerfully, a gift which, combined with his
natural quickness of humour, made him a powerful
force in politics and occasionally in the pulpit.

Reviewing a book published in 1802 by a French
author, a Monsieur Fievée under the title *Lettres sur
l'Angleterre*, Smith wrote:
   'Mr Fievée alleges against the English that they
have great pleasure in contemplating the spectacle of
men deprived of their reason. And indeed we must
have the candour to allow that the hospitality which
Mr Fievée experienced seems to afford some pretext
for this assertion.'

'I have to believe in the Apostolic Succession,' he once
confessed. 'There is no other way of explaining the
descent of the Bishop of Exeter from Judas Iscariot.'

In 1819 a book called *Anastasius; or, Memoirs of a
Modern Greek* rocked the literary world. Published
anonymously, it was universally accredited to Byron
because of its powers of imagination and description
and its obvious knowledge of the world. However,
when it was revealed that the book was actually the
work of one Thomas Hope, who until then had published nothing more daring than a book on indoor
decoration and a couple of works on ancient clothes,
the literary world was even more amazed. Not so
Sydney Smith, however. He commented in his review:
   'Mr Hope should avoid humour, in which he certainly does not excel. His attempts of that nature are
among the most serious parts of the book.'

Although not the most diligent of clergyman in his
religious duties Sydney Smith attended to his flock with
interest and concern. He was arguing once with a

doctor on the merits of their two professions, the doctor insisting that the work of Smith and men like him was largely wasted on those who were not devout by nature.

'You have to admit that your profession doesn't make angels of men,' he said, in conclusion.

'No,' Smith agreed. 'You doctors certainly have the best of us there.'

After a contemporary's long overdue demise he remarked:

'His was the sort of career which would make the recording angel think of taking up shorthand.'

'You must walk on an empty stomach,' Smith was once advised by his doctor.

'Whose?' he asked.

On boring sermons:

'Is sin to be taken from men, as Eve from Adam, by casting them into a deep slumber?'

Charles Maurice de Talleyrand Périgord
Talleyrand was one of those exciting figures in France at the turn of the nineteenth century who may not have been sure which way the wind was blowing but who successfully managed to sail with it. After serving Napoleon, and indeed helping to seize power, Talleyrand decided that the Empire was doomed and started communicating with the Allies. He was ultimately instrumental in restoring the Bourbon dynasty through subversion – what many chose to call treachery. And he did all this while being a bishop. Little wonder that Talleyrand has become known as one of the leading cynical wits of revolutionary France.

When a politician once asked him in despair how he could convert the peasants of France to rationalism, Talleyrand suggested:

'Well, you might try getting crucified and rising again on the third day.'

Defining love:
'That self-love *à deux*.'

When a friend defended the conduct of the upper chamber of government saying:
'At least you find consciences there.'
Talleyrand answered:
'Ah yes, many, many consciences. Semonville, for example, has at least two.'

On the famous writer Mme de Staël:
'She is such a good friend that she would throw all her acquaintances into water for the pleasure of fishing them out.'

Mme de Staël was holding forth on the advantages of the British constitution to a group of friends, when Talleyrand whispered to his neighbour:
'Above all she admires the habeas corpus.'

Commenting on another lady, whose amatory pursuits had been more successful than Mme de Staël's, Talleyrand said:
'Mme de Genlis, in order to avoid the scandal of coquetry, always yielded easily.'

Mme de Staël's most famous novel was *Delphine*, a book in which it was generally believed that the authoress had taken herself as model for the heroine and Talleyrand for one of the principal characters, an elderly matron. When they met for the first time after publication of the work, Talleyrand said to Mme de Staël:
"They tell me that we are both of us in your novel, in

the disguise of women.'

When someone remarked to Talleyrand that Joseph
Fouché, Napoleon's Minister of Police, had a profound
contempt for human nature, he replied:
'To be sure; he has made a careful study of himself.'

A diplomat told Talleyrand once that he couldn't
understand why people thought that he was ill-
natured, because he had never done more than one
ill-natured action in his whole life.
'And when will that end?' asked Talleyrand.

On François de Chateaubriand, a contemporary
politician:
'When he does not hear anyone talking about him, he
thinks he has gone deaf.'

Talleyrand suffered from slight lameness, an affliction
which many of his adversaries picked on when they
wanted to make fun of him. One day at court he hobbled
over to pay his respects to a lady for whom he had no
particular liking, and whose opinion of Talleyrand was
no higher.
'*Comment vous portez-vous*, Monsieur Talleyrand?'
asked the lady, deliberately using a phrase which
could either mean 'How are you?' or 'How do you carry
yourself?'
The lady herself was not without blemish – in fact,
she suffered from a slight squint – and Talleyrand,
realising her true meaning, replied:
'*Comme vous voyez, madame.*' which could either
mean: 'As you see, madam,' or 'In the same way that
you look, madam.'

Sir Herbert Beerbohm Tree
Tree was the half-brother of Max Beerbohm. He was
one of the leading actor-managers of the English stage,

an actor who excelled in character parts like Falstaff and Fagin, but who also essayed the great classical roles like Hamlet – in spite of W.S. Gilbert's remark that his Hamlet was 'Funny without being vulgar'.

He once returned the manuscript of a play to its hopeful author with the note that read:

> 'My dear Sir:
> I have read your play.
> Oh, my dear Sir!
> Yours faithfully,
> Beerbohm Tree.'

Rehearsing a new production on the stage of his theatre, His Majesty's, he asked one of the young actors to move back a little. The man did so and the rehearsal continued. A few lines later, Tree stopped the scene again and asked the man to step back a little more, which again he did. When, however, Tree stopped the scene again to ask the man to step even further, he protested:
'If I go back any further, I shall be right off the stage.'
'Yes,' said Tree, 'that's right', and turned back to his script.

In an effort to persuade a popular actor to rejoin his company, Tree invited the man into his dressing-room one evening as he was making up, to discuss terms,
'How much would you want to come back?' he asked.
The man named his price and, without looking up, Tree said to him:
'Don't slam the door when you go out, will you?'

Tree was entertaining Giovanni Grasso, the highly volatile Italian actor, during one of his visits to London. He came to watch Grasso's performance in the evening and then waited for him backstage after the show. Grasso finally emerged from his dressing-room and proceeded to embrace everyone between there and the stage door. He was just about to get into the car to go to Tree's supper party, when he suddenly dashed back into the theatre, which surprised everyone except Tree who remarked:

'He has forgotten to kiss the fireman.'

Mark Twain
A unique cross between George Bernard Shaw and Abraham Lincoln, Twain was a man from the frontier-lands of the mid-west whose reputation as a humorous and satirical writer established him as a major literary figure in the last quarter of the nineteenth century, bringing a taste of frontier earthiness to the growing canon of American literature.

Discussing old masters:
'If old masters had labelled their fruit, one wouldn't be so likely to mistake pears for turnips.'

Asked about a recently deceased politician, Twain said:
'I did not attend his funeral; but I wrote a nice letter saying that I approved of it.'

Twain went to borrow a book from one of his neighbours. The neighbour said that he was more than welcome to read it, but added:
'I must ask you to read it here. You know I make it a rule never to let any book go out of my library.'

A few days later the same neighbour came to Mark Twain's house to ask if he could borrow his lawn-mower.

'Certainly,' he said, 'but I must ask you to use it here. You know I make it a rule.'

Twain and the novelist and critic William Dean Howells were leaving church one morning as it started to rain heavily.

'Do you think it will stop?' asked Howells.

'It always has,' answered Twain.

A Mormon friend of Mark Twain tackled him once on the topic of polygamy and proceeded to harangue him with dogma and self-justification. He finally challenged him to cite any passage in the Bible that expressly forbade polygamy.

'Nothing easier,' said Twain. 'No man can serve two masters.'

Whistler invited Twain to visit his studio one day and look over the paintings he had there. Coming across one large, impressive canvas, still mounted on an easel, he moved his hand across the surface to feel the texture of the paint.

'Don't touch that,' cried Whistler. 'Can't you see, it isn't dry yet?'

'I don't mind,' said Twain. 'I have gloves on.'

On Cecil Rhodes:

'I admire him, I frankly confess it; and when his time comes I shall buy a piece of the rope for a keepsake.'

On Wagner:

'Wagner's music is better than it sounds.'

During one of his visits to England, Mark Twain was the guest of an old-established family in the country. His host showed him round the ancient manor with great pride. He pointed out the various periods in which the house had been built and finished his tour in the medieval hall which was hung with a large picture depicting the trial of Charles I. Pointing to one of the least notable figures to the side of the painting, he said with undisguised pride:

'An ancestor of mine.'

Twain nonchalantly pointed his finger at one of the

judges presiding over the trial and calmly said:

'An ancestor of mine but it is no matter, I have others.'

Moving on to France, Twain stayed with Paul Bourget, the leading French novelist and Academician, with whom he had another set-to on ancestry.

'Life can never be entirely dull to an American,' Bourget told him patronisingly. 'When he has nothing else to do he can always spend a few years trying to discover who his grandfather was.'

'Right, your Excellency,' said Twain, 'But I reckon a Frenchman's got a little standby for a dull time too; he can turn in and see if he can find out who his father was.'

A visitor to Mark Twain's own home complained to him about the untidy state of his books which were scattered all round the house, many of them piled on top of each other on the floor. He asked why things had got so bad and Mark Twain told him coldly:

'You see, it's so very difficult to borrow shelves.'

A sanctimonious citizen of Boston, with an immoral reputation that far from matched his feigned piousness, told Mark Twain:

'I intend to go to the Holy Land before I die and recite the Ten Commandments on Mount Sinai.'

'Really?' said Twain. 'Why not stay here in Boston and keep them?'

Twain was the guest of a Boston art patron one evening shortly after an auction at which the man had paid a huge sum of money for a Renaissance sculpture of a young woman coiling her hair. The proud owner showed his latest acquisition to his guest saying:

'There, what do you think of that?'

'It isn't true to nature,' said Twain, after looking carefully at the bust.

'Why not?' asked the horrified owner.

'She ought to have her mouth full of hairpins,' said Twain.

Twain was once invited to join a party at the opera in New York to hear a performance of *La Traviata*. The performance was everything he hoped it would be, except that his hostess spent the entire evening talking and whispering to the famous writer, so that he found it impossible to concentrate on the singing. As they were applauding the cast at the final curtain, the lady said effusively:

'Oh, I do so want you to be with us next Friday evening. I'm certain you will like it – the opera will be *Tosca*.'

'Charmed, I'm sure,' replied Twain. 'I've never heard you in that.'

'Whoever has lived long enough to find out what life is, knows how deep a debt of gratitude we owe to Adam, the first great benefactor of our race. He brought death into the world.'

'We like the people who say straight out what they think – provided they think the same as us.'

François Marie Arouet de Voltaire
Voltaire was a motive force in the movement in eighteenth-century France which I was always told was called the 'enlightenment'. He was a universal literary genius and excelled as a dramatist, an historian, a philosopher and a poet. His art was often directed to exposing and ridiculing the sick state of the society in which he lived.

Voltaire and the Earl of Chesterfield were together at a ball in London, standing by the side of the ballroom watching the guests. One glossy beauty, heavy with wig and make-up, paid great attention to the famous

114

French visitor. Chesterfield noticed her attentions and warned Voltaire jokingly:

'Sir, take care that you are not captivated.'

'My lord,' said Voltaire, 'I scorn to be taken by an English craft with French colours.'

Voltaire's great literary contemporary, Denis Diderot, was held in great esteem as a philosopher and wit, even by Voltaire, although the latter's appreciation had a sting in the tail:

'Diderot is a great wit and conversationalist,' he affirmed, 'but nature has denied him one great gift – that of dialogue.'

When Jean Baptiste Rousseau published his ode *To Posterity* Voltaire dismissed it with the remark:

'This poem will not reach its destination.'

On the Holy Roman Empire:

'The conglomeration which was called and still calls itself the Holy Roman Empire was not Holy, nor Roman, nor was it in any way an Empire.'

James McNeill Whistler

Whistler was an American artist and acid wit who settled in London and became a member of the glittering bohemian set caricatured in Gilbert and Sullivan's *Patience*. In 1890 he published a book with an unforgettable title: *The Gentle Art of Making Enemies*.

An American lady asked him once where he had been born.

'In Lowell, Massachusetts,' he told her.

'Why, Mr Whistler, whatever possessed you to be born in a place like that?' she said sardonically.

'The explanation is quite simple, madam,' he replied.

'I wished to be near my mother.'

Whistler's views on art did not extend to an admiration of the works of the landscape painter J.M.W. Turner. When an excited lady came to him with the news that her husband had unearthed what he thought were a couple of Turners in a junk shop, Whistler wasn't in the least interested.

'Would you be kind enough to come and tell us whether you think they're genuine or imitation Turners?' she asked.

'Madam,' said Whistler, 'that's a fine distinction.'

When a wealthy art patron asked Whistler's advice on which of his collection he should leave as a bequest to charity, Whistler told him:

'I should leave them to an asylum for the blind.'

Once he'd become an established figure in artistic circles Whistler was frequently approached by fellow artists with requests for help. He agreed to help one man in getting his painting hung in one London exhibition, but when they went to see it, the artist was horrified to see that his masterpiece had been hung upside down.

'Ssh,' Whistler whispered to him, 'the committee refused it the other way.'

When a client came to collect his portrait from Whistler and showed his dissatisfaction with the remark:

'Do you call that a good piece of art?'

Whistler retorted:

'Well, do you call yourself a good piece of nature?'

When a woman he met informed him that she had just travelled by train along the Thames valley and seen a view which reminded her of one of his paintings, Whistler told her:

'Yes, madam, nature is creeping up.'

Whistler was in Paris at the time of the coronation of King Edward VII and attended an ex-patriots' party to celebrate the event. One of the ladies present approached him and introduced herself by saying:

'I believe you know King Edward, Mr Whistler.'

'No, madam,' he replied.

'Why, that's strange.' said the lady, 'I met the King last year, and he said he knew you.'

'Oh that was just his brag,' said Whistler.

Whistler's habit of deliberately flouting any social or professional hierarchy occasionally backfired. His pet poodle developed a throat infection which threw Whistler into a panic and caused him to call in the country's leading throat specialist, Sir Morell Mackenzie, who later became infamous for his wrong diagnosis of the malignant condition of Frederick III of Germany. Mackenzie arrived and was less than amused to see that he'd been called to examine a dog. However, he looked into the poodle's mouth, wrote out a prescription and went away with his usual exorbitant fee. The next day Whistler received a message from the surgeon asking him to come to his house quickly. Whistler hurried round because he thought that there might have been a complication with his pet's infection, but when he arrived Mackenzie welcomed him saying:

'How do you do, Mr Whistler? I wanted to see you about having my front door painted.'

An international art competition held in Munich one year awarded Whistler its Gold Medal, Second Class. Writing to thank the Secretary, Whistler said:

'Pray convey my sentiments of tempered and respectable joy to the gentlemen of the Committee, and my

117

complete appreciation of the second-class compliment paid to me.'

And before we reach Wilde in his own right, here are two of Oscar's observations at Whistler's expense:
'Mr Whistler has always spelt art with a capital "I".'
'Popularity is the only insult that has not yet been offered to Mr Whistler.'

Oscar Wilde
Oscar Wilde needs no introduction. Mention the word 'wit' and his name automatically springs to mind. If any of us were asked which of the great wits of history we would like to have been, there can't be many who wouldn't include Wilde.

There are many examples of his gift at work. Here are some of my favourites:

'When the gods wish to punish us they answer our prayers.'

'Forty years of romance make a woman look like a ruin and forty years of marriage make her look like a public building.'

Writing a letter from America to a friend in England he commented on his companion:
'Frank Harris is upstairs thinking about Shakespeare at the top of his voice.'

'There are two ways of disliking poetry. One way is to dislike it, the other is to read Pope.'

'English actors act quite well, but they act best between the lines.'

On Frank Harris, his biographer as he then was:
'Every great man nowadays has his disciples, and it

is always Judas who writes his biography.'

And:

'Frank Harris is invited to all the great houses in England – once.'

On a book about Italian literature:

'A want of knowledge that must be the result of years of study.'

'Man is a reasonable animal who always loses his temper when he is called upon to act in accordance with the dictates of reason.'

After his success as Lord Illingworth, in Wilde's play *A Woman of No Importance*, Sir Herbert Beerbohm Tree started to conduct himself in the manner of the character and dropping witticisms as his lordship would. This drew the comment from Wilde:

'Ah, every day dear Herbert becomes *de plus en plus* Oscarisé; it is a wonderful case of nature imitating art.'

On George Meredith, the novelist:

'Who can define him? His style is chaos illuminated by flashes of lightning. As a writer he has mastered everything except language; as a novelist he can do everything except tell a story. As an artist he is everything except articulate.'

'Experience is the name everyone gives to his mistakes.'

'One can always be kind to people about whom one cares nothing.'

At the end of one of his lectures, Walter Pater was surrounded by a group of friends who congratulated him enthusiastically.

'I hope you were able to hear what I said,' said Pater.
'We overheard you,' said Wilde.

Once in a while, Wilde was the victim of the malicious wit of others. During one of his lectures in America, Wilde harangued his audience on their aesthetic immaturity and concluded his address with the derogatory pronouncement:

'And so Philistines have invaded the sacred sanctum of art!'

'I suppose that's why we're being assaulted with the jawbone of an ass,' said a voice from the audience.

And his brother, William Wilde, had this to say of him:

'Oscar was not a man of bad character; you could trust him with a woman anywhere.'

The Rules of Sarcasm

Learning all the greatest sarcastic lines in the world won't turn us into great practitioners of the art. There are do's and dont's for sarcasm as there are for every other human activity, and these play as important a part in the success of the sarcasm we use.

One of the most common mistakes that people make is to leave themselves open to a sarcastic retort after they've played their winning ace. It's like the tennis or squash player who stands admiring his or her shot at the back of the court and then fails to return the ball when it's miraculously retrieved by the opponent. Take this good example:

Not long after having failed to gain the hand of a dazzling Miss Steel, Robert Hall, the famous Baptist priest, was invited to take tea with a group of other ladies. Disappointed and offended by his evident lack of spirits in her company, Hall's hostess commented sourly:

'You are dull, Mr Hall, and we have no polished steel to brighten you with.'

'Oh, madam, that is of no consequence,' he replied. 'You have plenty of polished brass.'

No doubt in most other company the good lady's little, sneering jibe would have been highly effective. It was an elegant pun, it portrayed the young lady as being cold and hard, and it was carefully calculated to hurt Hall while also pointing out his apparent failure as a guest. It also took the form of an apology that implied that the ladies themselves were somehow to blame for his mood, which might reasonably have demanded some form of compliment to them.

Hall was too quick for her, however, and moved in for the kill, turning her remark into an open insult and responding with the same. Winning the point *and* the match.

So, in order to be effective, sarcasm has to hit its mark and annihilate first time, rather like duelling with a single shot in the pistol.

There *are* ways of ensuring that this happens and that's what these notes are concerned with. Choosing the target is the secret. Don't worry about playing fair – there aren't any Queensbury Rules in sarcasm. Just look for your opponent's most vulnerable spot, move in with your teeth and don't let go until you've won. Dogs and continentals fight like that and it's surprising how often they win.

Sarcasm and work
It doesn't really matter whereabouts you are in your particular profession or occupation, there's always a 'them' and an 'us'. The 'us' is usually underpaid, over-worked, misunderstood, exploited and downtrodden. The 'them' is the exact reverse.

Starting from this point of origin, any sarcasm can branch out along any of these fertile corridors of resentment and age-old rivalry. You'll never be short of supporters, providing you strike a common chord. After all, how often do we hear union bosses saying anything that goes against the grain with their members?

It's probably a fair guess that the idea of a man taking a pride in his work is a dead duck. Tell a car-worker that the car he's building is a load of rubbish and the chances are that he'll agree with you, pro-viding that he's not Japanese, of course.

No, any effective sarcasm has to be aimed at the

thing that he cherishes most. His money, perhaps? There again he'll only agree with you if you say that he's not worth half what he's paid. Providing the idiots at the top (which is gradually coming to mean the tax-payer) are prepared to keep coughing up the lolly, it's not his fault if he accepts it.

My feeling is that the only effective way is to go for what he regards as his sacrosanct wisdom, the belief that he is in control of what is happening to him. And this applies to everyone from Civil Servants right down to the Members of Parliament. None of us likes to feel that we are being manipulated in the way we spend a third of our lives. None of us likes to be told that what we believe to be our decisions are in fact made and programmed by other people. It's not even necessary to know who does pull the power strings. All that's required is to sew a few cankerous seeds of doubt and leave them to fester. How else do the unions work? How else for that matter does the government work? If we weren't all so busy blaming someone else, or the Japanese, for the mess we're in we might see the truth, whatever that is.

Sarcasm and authority
This one's got to be handled with a bit of care. Telling a policeman that he can't nail you for drunken driving because he isn't wearing his hat may not be the most appropriate way of getting off the charge, if the law's been changed. By virtue of being in an inferior position sarcasm has to be used with stealth and caution.

If, however, it's borne in mind that the essential requirement of sarcasm is to unsettle and irritate an opponent, then there are several ways of doing this effectively without the necessity of being overtly rude.

Take the bank manager, for instance. A visit to him is usually for only one thing at present. However, there's no need to let that dissuade you from sticking in the knife and giving a twist now and again. Remember, he does it all the time.

So, go in smiling and suddenly change your expression when you see his face. Don't let him open the conversation, start in right away with how ill he's looking. This will shake anyone who spends three afternoons out of five playing golf. (It has the added advantage of showing concern for his well-being, which is more than he does for yours, and might therefore moderate his opinion of you.)

Then, if he offers you a cigarette, either say that you've had to give up smoking to economise and pay the interest on your loan or, better still, decline it and say that you only smoke Havanas. While he's leading up to the reason he's hauled you in, have a quick glance round the office to see if there's anything new there since the last time you were in. New carpet? New telephone – one without a receiver perhaps that you just speak into? Any new gadgets spewing paper into the room? Any new drinks in evidence, more expensive whiskys? Have a good look and pounce on anything you see. Have a look at the man himself. How much did his suit cost? Is that a gold pen he's playing with? How recent is his suntan (in spite of what you said when you came in)? Are there any car-keys on the desk or did you notice a smart car outside? All these details may seem irrelevant, but when he starts in on you for living beyond your means and overspending, they're going to provide you with all the ammunition you need for hitting back at him along the lines that at least you're not living beyond other people's means, like he and the bank are.

Traffic wardens
Easier meat than bank managers but as infuriating as wasps when they sting you for six pounds for popping into the off-licence to buy the last of the pre-budget gin leaving the car sitting on the double-yellow lines outside.

125

Traffic wardens can usually be divided into two categories – men and women. (Though selective in-breeding and cloning seem to be producing a traffic warden breed of indeterminate sex but usually with bad complexions.)

Here again, start with feigned sympathy. Tell the warden that you think it's a disgrace that they (the 'them' factor in the world of traffic wardens) expect him or her to go out on duty dressed as they are. Pick on certain items of the uniform, the ones that look most ridiculous, like the hats or boots.

If you happen to be driving a foreign car point out how surprising it is they seem to have given tickets to all the people who didn't buy British Leyland or Ford (no one seems to be buying the other makes except Rolls-Royces, but then they never get booked anyway – money talks to wardens as it does to the rest of us). If, however, you've got a British car, point out that all the foreign cars seem to have been let off.

One of the easiest and most satisfying ways of getting in a sarcastic dig is to bait the warden. When you see one lurking round shop-doorways walk past calmly and then suddenly notice him or her. Grab the children if you've got them, or bundle up the shopping, and quicken your pace towards your car, throwing a few furtive glances over your shoulder. Any traffic warden worth his or her salt, and the bonus for booking an extra vehicle on the shift, will be after you like a grey-hound and will arrive at your car only a fraction of a second after you, pen poised ready to hand over the nasty little form. All you have to do then is to point to the meter, or whatever is measuring the length of your stay, and point out as caustically as you can that, unless you're very much mistaken, you've still got another ten minutes to run.

Sarcasm and the neighbours
Most of this book is devoted to illustrating how over the

ages men and women have succeeded in souring their relationships with their fellow human beings, but there is one brand of human being that requires a note all of its own, and that's the neighbour.

Second only to one's own family, the neighbour is probably the person one sees most of in life. So it's worth spending a little time working out the best ways of establishing a sarcastic superiority over him or her, should the need ever arise.

Again, aim for the object of the neighbour's pride. If he's a fanatic about looking after his car, point out that your own one is so good it doesn't require all the fiddling that he indulges in every weekend. Alternatively, pop round one day and say that you've seen an advert for a tremendous new rust-removing agent which you thought he might be interested in, since watching the job he did last week you reckon he'll be in for trouble come the winter.

If he's a great gardener you can either completely pave your own garden and sit in the sun all the time telling him he's a bloody fool sweating away when he could be enjoying himself. Or you can read up a few nasty diseases and then tell him airily one day that you think he's overlooked greenfly, or honey-fungus because it's raging in the district and killing off everything. (Just for good measure secretly tip half a pint of turps over the fence and let it kill off a wallflower or something to prove your point.)

If he takes a special pride in his vegetables try complimenting him on his excellent carrots when he's lifting some giant turnips for the local horticultural show. If he's a fruit man ask if he's thinking of having a go at growing strawberries the next time he proudly shows how his are getting on. And when he tells you that's what they are, say that you're sorry but you mistook them for raspberries.

All of these may seem petty, but if they get you started on a course of bad neighbour relations, it won't be long before you can really enjoy being at each others' throats properly.

Sarcasm and foreigners
This is one of the most difficult areas of sarcasm but one that offers the greatest potential if handled well. The essential problem is communication, by which I don't necessarily mean language since, with the right skills, language can be done away with when sarcasm takes over. Besides, unless you happen to be rather good at the language in question, trying to be sarcastic could land you in trouble if you make a mistake and end up looking a complete idiot.

My own policy is to play safe and stick to English, which immediately puts you at an advantage over the filthy wop or obese Aryan you're having a go at. There's no point trying to be subtle under these circumstances, though. To get the point across, the message has got to be clear and simple.

The war is usually good ammunition for getting in a first blow, and this even applies when talking to Americans, if you point out that their total involvement in both World Wars amounted to little more than half of ours, in terms of time at any rate.

You can try reminding the French about the Maginot Line that was going to stop any advance from the north. The Italians are such easy game that it's scarcely worth listing the openings their war record offers. The Germans have to be treated carefully. It's best to keep off the Nazis altogether. Just go for the military blunders, like forgetting about the Russian winter, or getting cold feet over the invasion of Britain. They're so sensitive on the whole issue that even a mild snub will produce very pleasing results.

The problem with being English now, of course, is that we make pretty good objects for sarcasm ourselves, with our weather, our economy, the state of the national football team and the quality of food everywhere between St. Ives and St. Andrews, particulary motorway catering. So, before wading in to complain about some aspect of continental life which has rubbed you up the wrong way, you'd be well advised to stop and check that your opponent can't come back with some even more telling remark about the British.

And this brings us back to the earlier note about the way that continentals fight. Now that we're part of the Common Market, it's not just trade that we've got to get better at. We've got to learn how to survive in the same way as nine other nations, all of which are reckoned to have achieved an acceptable state of civilisation. And that is why many of the examples given earlier come from continental sources. They do at least provide a convenient way in to the subject.

Flashes of Brilliance

The gift of sarcastic wit isn't confined to the great ones, of course. Politicians, clergymen, painters, musicians, writers, poets and peasants have all contributed to the canon of sarcastic lore. They may not immediately fall into the category of 'Noted Wits' but their own, occasional 'flashes of brilliance' are often more startling for their rarity.

As before, I haven't tried to classify this rich and varied section in any way. It's presented in a straightforward A-Z format so that you can select your own favourites and make your own judgements as to who is the best, the nastiest or the most devastating. The situations in which these *bon mots* were made and the circumstances that led up to them can be translated into our own lives in dozens of ways. Learning by example is the simplest way of learning. And when the examples are as entertaining as these, we can take a vicarious pleasure in cutting unseen enemies down to size, without running the risk of being gunned down ourselves.

Nearly all of the gems included here are attributed to a known source. However, there are a group at the end that cannot be rightly claimed by any one person. These are included because in a crisis they are just as useful as the others.

With all these stories there's no hard and fast guarantee that the name I've given is in fact that of the originator of the line. It's not uncommon to find the best of *bon mots* (the *mieux mots*?) attributed to more than one authority. For example, take Oscar Wilde's aphorism:

'In the world there are only two tragedies. One is not

getting what one wants and the other is getting it.'

And compare it with George Bernard Shaw's:

'There are two tragedies in life. One is not to get your heart's desire. The other is to get it.'

Who is to say which of the two originated the thought? Who is to say whether what is recorded is really a verbatim account, or one that's been improved with the passage of time?

You may believe that Bogart actually said 'Play it again, Sam,' when in fact he didn't, but whether he did or did not hardly matters. In the same way, whether the figures credited with one *bon mot* or another really said what is claimed is not the main issue. What counts is that the lines stand in their own right.

Franklin Pierce Adams

After seeing the actress Helen Hayes in a production of *Caesar and Cleopatra* Adams remarked that the Egyptian queen seemed to be suffering from:

'Fallen archness.'

Joseph Addison

Addison was a modest, unassuming man, who never pushed himself forward in company. This was often misunderstood and mistaken for arrogance and haughtiness. He was once accused by a leading lady, to whom he had been talking, of being dull and heavy in conversation:

'Madam, I have only ninepence in my pocket,' he told her coldly, 'but I can draw for a thousand pounds.'

Addison once loaned a sum of money to a friend with whom he was in the habit of having long, argumentative conversations. After the loan, Addison noticed that his friend ceased arguing with him, but lamely agreed with everything he said. When the debtor eventually took Addison's side on a matter which had previously had them both banging the table, Addison turned on him and said:

'Either contradict me, sir, or pay me my money.'

Fred Allen
Asked for his opinion of life in California by a friend who was contemplating the move west, Allen told him:

'Why, California's a fine place to live – if you happen to be an orange.'

Gracie Allen
'My husband will never chase another woman. He's too fine, too decent, too old.'

Sophie Arnoud
'Women give themselves to God when the Devil wants nothing to do with them.'

Nancy Astor
The Labour MP, Jimmy Thomas, was staying with the Astors during one of their famous Cliveden parties. His hostess asked what he would speak about if she asked him to address the party:

'How about my telling them what the Labour Party is going to do with this house, if it gets into power after the war?' he asked.

'My own suggestion,' said Lady Astor, moving in for the kill, 'is that you turn it into a boarding house and make me the landlady; though in that case, Mr Thomas, you'd have to pay for your board and lodging, which you've never done in the past.'

C.T. Atkinson
Atkinson was a notorious woman-hater, who, long after women were formally admitted to lectures, stubbornly refused to teach them. On one occasion, when he found half a dozen girls attending a lecture, he announced that he would begin by discussing the sexual prowess of natives of the Polynesian Islands. The girls hastily got up to leave but, as they were going

out of the door, Atkinson shouted after them:

'It's all right, ladies. You needn't rush. There isn't another boat for a month.'

Clement Attlee
On the House of Lords:

'The House of Lords is like a glass of champagne – that has stood for five days.'

A.J. Balfour
During his time as Prime Minister, Lord Balfour took part in a debate aimed at reducing the time spent discussing and arguing over parliamentary business on the floor of the House. Speaking against the motion, Sir Campbell Bannerman said that it was only reasonable that members should be permitted to let off 'a little intellectual steam'.

'Is that a polite way of describing the debating procedure of this house?' asked Balfour.

'I thought steam was a motive power,' continued Bannerman.

'Not when it is let off,' said Balfour sagely.

Elizabeth Barrett
She recorded her first meeting with William Wordsworth in the note:

'He was very kind to me and let me hear his conversation.'

Leonard Baskin
'Pop art is the inedible raised to the unspeakable.'

Cecil Beaton
On the mini-skirt:

'Never in the history of fashion has so little material been raised so high to reveal so much that needs to be covered so badly.'

*   *   *

Sarah Bernhardt
In 1915 the greatest *tragédienne* of the Edwardian stage had a leg amputated. While she was still recovering from the operation she received a telegram from the manager of the Pan-American Exposition asking if he could display her leg in San Francisco for a fee of £20,000.

'Which leg?' she replied.

Ambrose Bierce
On the fair sex:

'Here's to women! Would that we could fall into their arms without falling into their hands.'

'The gambling known as business looks with austere disfavour upon the business known as gambling.'

Marguerite, Countess of Blessington
Married at fourteen to a penniless army officer, later to a wealthy Earl, a friend of Byron and lastly forced to flee to Paris with a French Count, the Countess of Blessington could rightly claim to have knowledge of the world – a knowledge which led to a jaundiced view of romance.

'Love-matches,' she wrote, 'are made by people who are content, for a month of honey, to condemn themselves to a life of vinegar.'

Jacques Bossuet
As a leading churchman in seventeenth-century France, Bossuet was prohibited from marrying, which was just as well in view of his opinion of women:

'The cruellest revenge of a woman,' he wrote, 'is to remain faithful to a man.'

Heywood Broun
One of his jobs as a cub reporter was to interview the state legislator from Utah on a controversial issue to do

with the Mormon faith. The senator greeted the reporter pompously by telling him:

'Young man, I have nothing to say.'

'I know,' Broun replied. 'Now let's get down to the interview.'

John Mason Brown

After seeing one of Tallulah Bankhead's extravagant stage performances Brown wrote the notice:

'Miss Bankhead sailed down the Nile last night as Cleopatra – and sank.'

Pearl Buck

Speaking of the country in which she spent nearly forty years of her life, the novelist remarked sourly:

'We send missionaries to China so that the Chinese can get into heaven, but we don't let them into our country.'

Anthony Burgess

'Reviewers are not born but made, and they are made by editors.'

'Laugh and the world laughs with you. Snore and you sleep alone.'

George Burns

'My father used to take me to school. He had to – we were in the same class.'

Samuel Butler

'It was very good of God to let Carlyle and Mrs Carlyle marry one another and so make only two people miserable instead of four.'

Mrs Patrick Campbell

Speaking of a fellow actress:

'She is a great lady of the American stage. Her voice

is so beautiful that you won't understand a word she says.'

To the vegetarian Bernard Shaw:
  'Shaw, someday you'll eat beefsteak and then no woman in London will be safe.'

George Canning
To a vicar who asked how the Prime Minister enjoyed his sermon, Canning said:
  'You were brief.'
  'Yes,' said the vicar, 'you know that I avoid being tedious.'
  'But you were tedious,' added Canning.

Al Capp
On abstract art:
  'Abstract art: a product of the untalented, sold by the unprincipled to the utterly bewildered.'

Sir Edward Carson
Before becoming solicitor-general for Ireland, Carson established a formidable reputation for himself as prosecuting counsel.
  'Are you a teetotaller?' he asked one witness.
  'No, I'm not.'
  'Are you a moderate drinker?'
  No answer.
  'Should I be right if I called you a heavy drinker?'
  'That's my business.'
  'Have you any other business?'

Robert Carson
On television:
  'The longest amateur night in history.'

Joseph Chamberlain
During his time as mayor of Birmingham, Chamberlain

attended a number of civic functions in neighbouring cities. He had been invited to speak after a dinner at one of these and was looking forward to it until his host asked him:

'Shall we let them enjoy themselves a little longer, or had we better have your speech now?'

Coco Chanel

On Yves Saint Laurent:

'Saint Laurent has excellent taste. The more he copies me, the better taste he displays.'

Lord Chesterfield

During an argument Lord Chesterfield was told tartly that man was the only one of God's creatures endowed with the power of laughter.

'True,' replied Chesterfield, eyeing his opponent critically. 'And you may add, perhaps, that he is the only creature that deserves to be laughed at.'

G.K. Chesterton

'The Bible charges us to love our neighbours and our enemies; probably because they are usually the same people.'

'The success of the marriage comes after the failure of the honeymoon.'

Colley Cibber

Cibber was one of the most outspoken and outrageous poets laureate ever appointed. Mercilessly pilloried by Pope in the *Dunciad*, he was a sharp and caustic wit himself, a man who enjoyed being in the limelight and who was quick to eclipse anyone who threatened to oust him from it. He was attending a fashionable reception when the son of the King's printer, who amongst other perks enjoyed the monopoly of printing Bibles, appeared extravagantly clad in green and gold. The

dazzling youth attracted great attention, especially as he was totally unknown to those present. Whispers circulated to find out who he was, but the mystery was dispelled by Cibber's stage-whisper to his neighbour:

'Oh, don't you know him? It's young Bible, bound in calf and gilt, but not lettered.'

Henry Clay
Clay was an American politician and orator, whose own skill as a speaker made him intolerant of others who were prolix and dull. After complaining audibly about the speech made by a fellow member of the assembly, full of quotations and rhetorical tricks, the man turned to him and said:

'You, sir, speak for the present generation; but I speak for posterity.'

'Yes,' agreed Clay, 'and you seem resolved to speak until the arrival of your audience.'

Irving S. Cobb
'Middle age: when you begin to exchange your emotions for symptoms.'

Samuel Taylor Coleridge
Asked by a woman if he believed in ghosts, Coleridge told her:

'No, madam, I have seen too many to believe in them.'

Gabriele d'Annunzio
A letter was handed to d'Annunzio while he was living in France addressed: 'To Italy's Greatest Poet'. He declined to accept it on the grounds that he wasn't Italy's greatest poet – but the world's.

Benjamin Disraeli
'A visit to a country house is a series of meals mitigated by the new dresses of the ladies.'

* * *

Robert Donat
Shortly before his long awaited return to the stage, in the 1953 production of *Murder in the Cathedral*, Donat was having his hair cut by a barber. As the man was snipping away Donat suddenly had a terrible fit of asthmatic coughing, which lasted several minutes. As he finally regained his breath and settled back in the chair, the barber asked tentatively:

'What will happen if you have an attack on the stage, sir?'

'There will be no extra charge,' Donat told him.

Alexandre Dumas
The famous novelist was staying with an equally famous physician in his house in Marseilles. His host asked Dumas if he would write one of his witty improvisations in his visitors' book. Dumas agreed and wrote the following lines while the doctor looked on:

'Since Dr Gistal came to our town,

To cure diseases casual and hereditary,

The hospital has been pulled down . . .'

'You flatterer,' interrupted the delighted doctor.

'And we've made a larger cemetery,' concluded Dumas.

Dumas received a manuscript from an ambitious young writer who wanted the great man to become his collaborator in a forthcoming work.

'How dare you, sir, yoke together a noble horse and a contemptible ass?' wrote Dumas in indignation.

'How dare you, sir, call me a horse,' the young writer replied.

This pleased Dumas so much that he sent a further note saying:

'Send me your manuscript, my friend; I gladly accept your proposition.'

*   *   *

Finley Peter Dunne

The humorous critic, who wrote under the name of 'Mr Dooley', attended a performance given by Isadora Duncan, in which the dancer wore next to nothing. This, and the lighting, which reduced her covering even further, left little to the audience's imagination. Seeing Dunne leaving the theatre after the show, one of Isadora's fans asked him eagerly:

'Oh, Mr Dunne, how did you enjoy the madame's dancing?'

'Immensely,' he told her. 'It made me think of Grant's Tomb in love.'

Lord Ellenborough

Ellenborough was a judge not noted for sarcastic barbs, but sometimes he found them irresistible. On one occasion a barrister appearing before him spoke all day until four o'clock when he asked the judge when it would be 'the court's pleasure to hear the remainder of the argument'.

'We are bound to hear you, sir,' Ellenborough told him, 'and shall do so on Friday; but pleasure has long been out of the question.'

Inevitably Ellenborough didn't always have it his own way. He told one barrister:

'Sir, what you have been saying amounts almost to contempt of court.'

'With respect, my lord, I have not expressed any contempt but have been most careful to conceal it.'

Ralph Waldo Emerson

'The religion of one age is the literary entertainment of the next.'

'The virtues of society are the vices of the soul.'

*   *   *

William Faulkner
On Henry James:
   'Henry James was one of the nicest old ladies I ever met.'

Edna Ferber
Following a notice about a film based on one of her novels Edna Ferber wrote to the magazine editor:
   'Will you kindly inform the moron who runs your motion picture department that I did not write the movie entitled *Classified*? Neither did I write any of its wise-cracking titles. Also inform him that Moses did not write the motion picture entitled *The Ten Commandments*.'

Eugene Field
Reviewing a production of *King Lear*:
   'The actor who took the role of King Lear played the King under the momentary apprehension that someone else was about to play the ace.'

W.C. Fields
Asked if he had the DTs since coming to Hollywood:
   'I don't know. There's no way of telling where the DTs leave off and Hollywood begins.'

Scott Fitzgerald
Describing Ernest Hemingway:
   'Always willing to lend a helping hand to the one above him.'

Michael Foot
Speaking at the time of the Profumo scandal:
   'The members of our security services have apparently spent so much time looking under the beds for communists, they haven't had time to look in the bed.'

Samuel Foote
The eighteenth-century playwright and wit once asked

a friend why he continually sang the same tune.

'Because it haunts me,' the friend said.

'Little wonder', said Foote. 'You continually murder it.'

Foote and a group of friends were mulling over the latest gossip when the forthcoming marriage of a notorious lady of the town came up. One of them mentioned that the bride-to-be had made a full confession of her previous amours to her future husband.

'What honesty she must have,' said one of them.

'What courage,' said another.

'What a memory,' added Foote.

A blissfully happy man confided in Foote that he had just spent a thousand pounds on his 'dear wife'.

'She is indeed your dear wife,' Foote told him reprovingly.

Corey Ford
A woman wrote to Corey Ford once with a very simple message:

'I hope you stay single and make some poor girl happy.'

Charles James Fox
As a young man Fox ran up huge debts which caused his father to ask him how he was able to sleep or enjoy life when he considered the size of the amount he owed.

'Your lordship need not be in the least surprised,' Fox told him. 'Your astonishment ought to be how my creditors can sleep.'

Benjamin Franklin
Writing to William Strahan:

'You and I were long friends; you are now my enemy, and I am

Yours,
B. Franklin.'

Robert Frost
'A mother takes twenty years to make a man of her son, and another woman makes a fool of him in twenty minutes.'

'The world is full of willing people, some willing to work, the rest willing to let them.'

'The brain is a wonderful organ; it starts working the moment you get up in the morning and it does not stop until you get into the office.'

'By working faithfully eight hours a day, you may eventually get to be boss and work twelve hours a day.'

R. Buckminster Fuller
'Love is a many-splintered thing.'

Dr John Fuller
'A fool's paradise is a wise man's hell.'

Zsa Zsa Gabor
'A man in love is incomplete until he has married. Then he's finished.'

'I have never hated a man enough to give his diamonds back.'

'I haven't known any open marriages, though quite a few have been ajar.'

'I am a marvellous housekeeper. Every time I leave a man, I keep his house.'

*　　*　　*

'You never really know a man until you have divorced him.'

John Kenneth Galbraith
'Nothing is so admirable in politics as a short memory.'

Samuel Goldwyn
'Ninety per cent of the art of living consists in getting on with people that one cannot stand.'

Princess Grace of Monaco
'The freedom of the press works in such a way that there is not much freedom from it.'

Horace Greeley
'I am a self-made man,' one of his opponents told the nineteenth-century American politician during a row on the pros and cons of slavery, against which Greeley was a powerful campaigner.

'I'm glad to hear it,' Greeley told him. 'That, sir, relieves the Almighty of a great responsibility.'

Russell Green
'More hearts were served in the kitchen than were ever united at the altar.'

Jo Grimond
When Sir Alec Douglas Home's speechwriter, Mr Eldon Griffiths, became an MP and made his maiden speech in the Commons, the then Liberal leader, Jo Grimond, commented afterwards:

'We should perhaps commiserate with the Prime Minister at having lost a pen, though he may have gained a voice.'

Percy Hammond
Reviewing a musical:
'I have knocked everything but the knees of the

148

chorus girls, and nature has anticipated me there.'

Gilbert Harding
Asked by Mae West's manager if he could try to sound sexier during a radio interview with her, Harding replied:
'If, sir, I was endowed with the power of conveying unlimited sexual attraction through the potency of my voice, I would not be reduced to accepting a miserable pittance from the BBC for interviewing a faded female in a damp basement.'

Sir Cedric Hardwicke
In answer to the question:
    'How do you choose a part?'
    'I read the contract first.'

Jascha Heifetz
Expressing his views on modern music:
'I occasionally play works by contemporary composers and for two reasons. First to discourage the composer from writing any more, and secondly to remind myself how much I appreciate Beethoven.'

Heinrich Heine
Defining silence:
    'A conversation with an Englishman.'

Asked why he had left all his investments and possessions to his wife on the sole condition that she remarried after his death, he replied:
'When Matilda remarries, there will be at least one man who will regret my death.'

Bishop Hensley Henson
Bishop Henson paid a visit to his fellow ecclesiastic, Archbishop Cosmo Gordon Lang, not long after Lang had commissioned a portrait of himself. Showing

149

I WON'T TELL YOU AGAIN, DEAR, STOP
KICKING MY LATE HUSBAND'S HEADSTONE.

Henson the picture, Lang asked him what he thought of it. Politely, Henson first asked Lang what his own opinion was.

'I fear it portrays me as proud, arrogant and worldly,' he confessed.

'To which of the three does your Grace take exception?' Henson asked.

Oliver Herford
'Perhaps it was because Nero played the fiddle that they burned Rome.'

Enjoying a quiet lunch one day, Herford was infuriated by a man whom he particularly disliked coming up and slapping him on the back with the cheery greeting:

'Hello, Ollie, old boy, how are you doing?'

'I don't know your name, and I don't know your face,' Herford told the man acidly, 'but your manners are very familiar.'

Alfred Hitchcock
Hitchcock was once entertained to a very meagre dinner in which he was only offered miniscule portions in comparison with those he was used to consuming. His hostess did not appear to notice her guest's obvious dissatisfaction and when they were drinking their coffee she said cheerily to him:

'I do hope that you will soon dine here again.'

'By all means,' Hitchcock replied. 'Why don't we start now?'

William Hogarth
The famous painter and caricaturist was once commissioned by a tight-fisted client to paint a huge mural on his staircase of the destruction of the pharaoh's hosts in the Red Sea. The negotiations over the price were so long-winded and tedious that in the end Hogarth accepted the commission for a good half of

what it should have cost. He set to work and after only a couple of days informed his client that the job was finished, which surprised him. He was even more surprised when he saw that the entire wall was painted red.

'What have you here?' he asked. 'I ordered a scene of the Red Sea.'

'That you have,' said Hogarth.

'But where are the Israelites?'

'They are all gone over.'

'And where are all the Egyptians?'

'They are all drowned,' Hogarth told him triumphantly.

William Dean Howells

This famous American man of letters was once asked by a would-be poet if he would read through one of his compositions. Howells agreed, and when the young man returned to find out what he thought of it, Howells was full of praise.

'This is a magnificent poem,' he said. 'Did you write it unaided?'

'Yes, sir, every word,' the poet told him.

'Then I am very glad to meet you, Lord Byron, since I was under the impression that you had died a good many years ago at Missolonghi.'

J.B. Hughes

'If Moses had been a committee, the Israelites would still be in Egypt.'

Harold Ickes

When Thomas Dewey ran for the Republican nomination as Presidential candidate, at what was regarded as a very young age, the then Secretary of the Interior, Harold Ickes, dismissed his chances with the remark:

'I see that Dewey has thrown his diaper into the ring.'

Sir Henry Irving
Irving hated amateur actors and amateur theatricals.
Much against his better judgement he allowed himself
to be talked into sitting through a non-stop amateur
production of *Twelfth Night*. Immediately after the
curtain had fallen the excited director rushed round to
ask Irving what he'd thought of the production.

'Capital! Capital!' he replied. 'Where's the lava-
tory?'

Holbrook Jackson
'Love is the most subtle form of self-interest.'

M. Walthall Jackson
'One reassuring thing about modern art is that things
can't be as bad as they are painted.'

Franklin Pierce Jones
'The most difficult year of marriage is the one you're
in.'

'An extravagance is anything you buy that is of no
earthly use to your wife.'

James Joyce
Joyce was asked once whether he would ever consider
becoming a Protestant, having left the Catholic Church.

'I may have lost my faith,' he replied, 'but I haven't
lost my commonsense.'

George S. Kaufman
Commenting on Raymond Massey's performance as the
lead in the film *Abe Lincoln in Illinois*:

'Massey won't be satisfied until he's assassinated.'

Describing the work of an author who had become
notorious for his social critiques:

'He's in the chips now – but most of them seem to have stayed on his shoulders.'

He sent a telegram to the actor William Gaxton during the run of Kaufman's show, *Of Three I Sing*:
'I'm watching your performance from the rear of the house. Wish you were here.'

Walter Kerr
'Half the world is composed of idiots, the other half of people clever enough to take indecent advantage of them.'

Ernie Kovacs
On television:
'A medium, so called because it is neither rare nor well done.'

Henry Labouchère
As a young man, Labouchère worked in the Victorian version of the diplomatic corps, serving for a time as an attachè at the Russian court at St. Petersburg. One day a very pompous nobleman called at the British Legation and demanded to see the ambassador immediately.
'Pray take a chair,' Labouchère told him politely.
'But, young man, do you know who I am?' said the outraged visitor, who then reeled off his numerous titles and honours.
When he finished, Labouchère bowed his head in acknowledgement and said:
'In that case, pray take two chairs.'

Back in London he was amusing himself with a friend in the smoking-room of his club, telling racy stories about leading figures in the diplomatic and political world. The irreverent conversation of the two young men offended one of the older men present to such an extent that in the end he rose from his chair by the fire and stormed over to where they were sitting.

'Do you realise, sir,' he said angrily to Labouchère, 'that I knew your grandmother?'

'I had no idea, sir,' said Labouchère, politely rising to his feet and adding:

'Do I, perhaps, have the honour of addressing my grandfather?'

He remarked sardonically of one of the military leaders of his time, that the Duke of Cambridge was:

'Standing at the head of his troops, his drawn salary in his hand.'

Walter Savage Landor
'Ambition is but Avarice on stilts and masked.'

David Lardner
On a new play:
'The plot was designed in a light vein that somehow became varicose.'

Leslie Lever
'I have been accused of being ungenerous to this government,' the Labour MP once admitted. 'Generosity is part of my character, and I, therefore, hasten to assure this government that I will never make an allegation of dishonesty against it whenever a simple explanation of stupidity will suffice.'

Max Lieberman
Trying to concentrate on his subject's portrait, in spite of her perpetual talking, the famous German painter finally gave up his struggle and told her:
'One more word out of you and I'll paint you as you are.'

*   *   *

A.J. Liebling
'Freedom of the press is limited to those who own one.'

Hendrick van Loon
'Nothing is ever accomplished by a committee unless it consists of three members, one of whom happens to be sick and the other absent.'

H. Lawrence Lowell
'The present state of an MP's soul is conditioned by the future state of his seat.'

Clare Boothe Luce
'Censorship, like charity, should begin at home; but, unlike charity, it should end there.'

Eugene McCarthy
'We don't declare war any more; we declare national defence.'

Thomas Babington Macaulay
During an election campaign in Edinburgh, Macaulay found himself standing next to his opponent on a balcony one evening when he was suddenly struck by a dead cat, thrown by someone in the crowd. The man who threw the cat shouted out an apology to Macaulay, to the effect that he had intended the missile for his opponent.

'In that case,' said Macaulay, 'I wish you had meant it for me and struck him.'

Expressing his opinion of the Greek philosopher, Socrates:

'The more I read him, the less I wonder that they poisoned him.'

Anselm J. McLaurin
Commenting on his political opposition the senator said:

'The basic principle that will ultimately get the Republican Party together is the cohesive power of public plunder.'

Norman Mailer
'The function of socialism is to raise suffering to a higher level.'

W. Somerset Maugham
During a discussion on Christian morality, Somerset Maugham commented:
'You know of course that the Tasmanians, who never committed adultery, are now extinct.'

Lord Melbourne
On Macaulay:
'I wish I was as cocksure of anything as Tom Macaulay is of everything.'

Robert Mitchum
When asked: 'What do you look for in a good script?'
He answered: 'Days off.'

William Morris
On his first visit to Paris after the completion of the Eiffel Tower in 1889, the painter and poet William Morris spent most of his daylight hours in the restaurants in the Tower, eating his meals there and doing much of his work as well.
'You're certainly impressed with the Tower, monsieur,' one of the staff told him after he'd been there for about a week.
'Impressed?' said Morris. 'I stay here because it's the only place in Paris where I can avoid seeing the damned thing.'

Wolfgang Amadeus Mozart
A young composer visited Mozart and asked Mozart

how to set about writing a symphony.

'You're very young,' Mozart told him. 'Why not start by composing ballads?'

'But you composed symphonies when you were only ten years old.'

'I know,' replied Mozart, 'but I didn't ask "how?".'

George Nathan
When a friend showed George Nathan the picture of Mae West posing as the Statue of Liberty, freeing her fellow Americans from their moral inhibitions, Nathan commented:

'She looks more like the Statue of Libido.'

Beverley Nichols
'Marriage is a book in which the first chapter is written in poetry and the remaining chapters in prose.'

Friedrich Wilhelm Nietzsche
'Woman was God's second mistake.'

'Marriage makes an end of short follies, being one long stupidity.'

Sir Fletcher Norton
Norton was famous for his rudeness both in and out of the courtroom. In one case he appeared before Lord Mansfield and argued some intricate point of law relating to manors.

'My lord, I can illustrate the point in an instance in my own person,' he volunteered. 'I myself have two little manors.'

'We all know it, Sir Fletcher,' the judge told him.

Ignace Paderewski
The great Polish pianist was once invited by a wealthy young woman to give her a private concert. Knowing little of music herself she invited Paderewski to make

his own selection, which he did to her evident satisfaction. After he had finished one piece she asked
him:

'What a beautiful piece of music, who composed it?'

'Beethoven, madam,' Paderewski replied.

'Ah, yes,' she said, as if suddenly remembering, 'and
is he composing now?'

'No, madam, he is not,' said Paderewski. 'He is
decomposing.'

Thomas Love Peacock

'I hold that there is every variety of natural capacity,
from the idiot to Newton and Shakespeare; the mass of
mankind, midway between these extremes, being
blockheads of different degrees: education leaving
them pretty nearly as it found them, with this single
difference, that it gives a fixed direction to their
stupidity, a sort of incurable wry-neck to the thing they
call understanding. So one nose points always east,
another always west, and each is ready to swear that it
points due north.'

Dr Laurence Peter

'Slump and the world slumps with you. Push and you
push alone.'

'Only a mediocre person is always at his best.'

Alexander Pope

'The greatest advantages I know of being thought a wit
by the world is that it gives me the greater freedom of
playing the fool.'

Pope had the tables turned on him by a young man with
whom he was talking, and at whose ignorance Pope
sneered when he asked if he knew what an interro-
gation was and received the reply:

'Yes, sir, 'tis a little crooked thing that asks questions.'

Thomas Brackett Reed
Reed was Speaker of the House of Representatives in the American Congress in the last half of the nineteenth century. During his time in the chair he developed a formidable reputation for cutting speakers down to size with his caustic wit. One of the members of the house, from the state of Illinois, was arguing vehemently on one occasion:

'I'm right. I know I'm right, so I say, with Henry Clay, sir, I would rather be right than be President.'

'The gentleman from Illinois will never be either,' retorted Reed.

Speaking more generally on some of the members, he made the memorable comment:

'They never open their mouths without subtracting from the sum of human knowledge.'

Antoine de Rivarol
An over-enthusiastic poet asked the distinguished French writer to assess a couplet he had written. Rivarol read the two lines of verse through several times and handed them back to their composer with the remark:

'Very nice, though there are dull stretches.'

Samuel Rogers
The nineteenth-century writer and publisher Charles Knight had the reputation of being a great talker and an indifferent, not to say impatient, listener. When Samuel Rogers heard from a mutual acquaintance that Knight was beginning to go deaf, his only comment was:

'It is from lack of practice.'

*   *   *

Gioacchino Rossini
On Richard Wagner's music:
'Wagner had beautiful moments but awful quarter hours.'

Helen Rowland
'A fool and her money are soon courted.'

Lord Salisbury
Teasing him that a bishop was a man of greater authority than a judge, a friend said:
'A judge can do no more than say "You be hanged". A bishop has the power to say, "You be damned".'
'That may be true,' said Salisbury, 'but when a judge says "You be hanged", you are hanged.'

Sir Malcolm Sargent
While rehearsing for a performance of Handel's *Messiah*, Sir Malcolm Sargent stopped the orchestra and took the women's section of the chorus to task over the way they were singing *For Unto Us a Child is Born*.
'Just a little more reverence, please, and not so much astonishment,' he said by way of guidance.

On his seventieth birthday he was asked to what factor he contributed his advanced age, a question which drew the reply:
'Well, I suppose I must attribute it to the fact that I haven't died yet.'

Artur Schopenhauer
'What men commonly call their fate is mostly only their own foolishness.'

Madame de Sévigné
When a very attractive, but equally tedious, friend complained to the seventeenth-century lady of letters,

that she was being tormented by her lovers, Mme de Sévigné advised her:

'Oh madame, it is very easy to get rid of them, you have only to open your mouth.'

Richard Brinsley Sheridan
When Lord Lauderdale was about to repeat a joke which had greatly amused him, Sheridan butted in with the remark:

'For God's sake, don't, my dear Lauderdale; a joke in your mouth is no laughing matter.'

Robert Sherwood
On the cowboy film star, Tom Mix:

'They say he rides like part of the horse, but they don't say which part.'

John Simon
On Camelot:

'This film is the Platonic idea of boredom, roughly comparable to reading a three-volume novel in a language of which one knows only the alphabet.'

On Peter Sellers in *The World of Henry Orient*:

'Peter Sellers is such an experienced impersonator that one regrets his inability to add to his list of impressions the Peter Sellers that was.'

On Dore Schary, the American writer-producer:

'A man whose few successes were even more distasteful than his many failures.'

Philip Slater
'Insurance is death on the instalment plan.'

Dr Robert South
Dr South, like many clergymen in the second half of the seventeenth century, found preaching a

soul-destroying process. He found himself addressing the King, Charles II, and a number of his courtiers only to watch them slowly nodding off to sleep. When this lack of proper attention finally became intolerable Dr South departed from his text and said to one of the culprits:

'Lord Lauderdale, let me entreat you rouse yourself. You snore so loud that you will wake the King.'

Madame de Staël

While she was writing her memoirs a lady friend asked the renowned writer how she was able to portray herself and her amours.

'Oh, I shall give only a bust of myself,' replied the authoress.

Thaddeus Stevens

Abraham Lincoln asked Stevens whether the politician Simon Cameron was an honest man.

'He wouldn't steal a red-hot stove,' Stevens told the President.

Later he was challenged by one of Cameron's supporters over this decidedly ambivalent statement, and he finally withdrew the remark saying:

'I said that Cameron wouldn't steal a red-hot stove. I now withdraw that statement.'

Not long before his death, Stevens was visited by a group of colleagues who came to see how he was. One of them made a comment on his appearance which drew the characteristic response from the sick man, in spite of his illness:

'Ah, gentleman, it is not my appearance that I am concerned about just now, but my disappearance.'

Tom Stoppard

'Revolution is a trivial shift in the emphasis of suffering.'

*   *   *

Dr W.H. Thompson

The famous nineteenth-century classical scholar, Dr W.H. Thompson, once put a younger member of his college in place with the caustic remark:

'We are none of us infallible – not even the youngest among us.'

His fellow historian, Oscar Browning, complained to Thompson once that he had so many books he didn't know what to do with them. Thompson volunteered the idea that he might read some of them.

Jeremy Thorpe

When Prime Minister Harold Macmillan axed half his cabinet, the Liberal politician made the classic comment:

'Greater love hath no man than this, that he lay down his friends for his life.'

James Thurber

The cartoonist attended one of Hollywood's glossiest film premières and came out feeling cheated.

'I thought it stank,' his friend said. 'What did you think of it?'

'I can't say that I liked it that well,' said Thurber.

Lily Tomlin

'If love is the answer, could you rephrase the question?'

Joseph Turner

Turner wasn't noted for his tolerance and when it came to suffering self-opinionated ladies who talked nineteen-to-the-dozen about 'the great masters', his patience was virtually non-existent. When one of these unfortunates was holding forth at length one day about the merits of Cimabue, Turner stopped her in midsentence with the question:

'Do you seriously think, your ladyship, that any of his works can compare with those of the great Florentine, Mortadella da Bologna?'

'But how much better is Cimabue's colour!' exclaimed the lady.

'Not if you are a connoisseur of Italian sausages, madame,' Turner replied.

Kenneth Tynan
On a musical:
'It contains a number of those tunes one goes into the theatre humming.'

Evelyn Waugh
On an operation recently undergone by Randolph Churchill, father of Sir Winston:
'A triumph of modern science to find the only part of Randolph that wasn't malignant and remove it.'

Orson Welles
During a lecture tour the great director and film star found himself addressing a tiny audience in a remote town in the midwest. Unperturbed by the emptiness of the hall he followed his regular pattern which began with an outline of his work.

'I am a director of plays, a producer of plays. I am an actor of the stage and motion pictures. I'm a writer and a producer of motion pictures. I write, direct and act on the radio. I'm a magician and painter. I've published books. I play the violin and the piano.' Then, stopping to look at his audience, he added:

'Isn't it a pity there's so many of me and so few of you.'

*   *   *

Billy Wilder
On Charlie Chaplin:
'When he found a voice to say what was on his mind, he was like a child of eight writing lyrics for Beethoven's Ninth.'

On Spyros Skouras, president of Twentieth Century Fox for nearly twenty years:
'The only Greek tragedy I know is Spyros Skouras.'

On television:
'A twenty-one-inch prison. I'm delighted with it because it used to be that films were the lowest form of art. Now we have something to look down on.'

During the filming of *Sunset Boulevard*, Wilder, who was the director and writer of the film, said to his cameraman:
'Johnny, keep it out of focus. I want to win the foreign picture award.'

Michael Wilding
On actors:
'You can pick out actors by the glazed look that comes into their eyes when the conversation wanders away from themselves.'

John Wilkes
Wilkes was asked by a Roman Catholic to justify the Anglican religion.
'Where was your faith before Luther?' he jeered.
'Did you wash your face this morning?' Wilkes asked him in reply.
'That I did, sir.'
'Then pray where was your face before it was washed?' asked Wilkes in conclusion.

Earl Wilson
'A vacation is what you take when you can no longer

take what you've been taking.'

Woodrow Wilson
During one of his terms as governor of New Jersey, Wilson received a phone call telling him of the sudden death of a great friend of his in the Congress. He was still getting over the shock of this news when the phone rang again and another New Jersey politician said to him:

'Governor, I would like to take the Senator's place.'

'Well,' Wilson answered, 'you may quote me as saying that's perfectly agreeable to me if it's agreeable to the undertaker.'

Walter Winchell
'Nothing recedes like success.'

Peggy Wood
The actress Peggy Wood joined a conversation in which Alexander Woollcott, the Falstaffian drama critic, was airing the possibility of reviving *Macbeth* on Broadway.

'We're discussing the cast,' he told her, 'but I don't think you'd make a very good Lady Macbeth, do you, Peggy?'

'No, Alec,' she said. 'But you would.'

Alexander Woollcott
Woollcott went back to a college reunion, against his better judgement, and, as he feared, was approached by a face all too memorable.

'Hello, Alex. You remember me, don't you?' said the face.

'I can't remember your name, but don't tell me,' said Woollcott.

On Harold Ross, editor of the *New Yorker*:

'Ross has the utmost contempt for anything he doesn't understand.'

*   *   *

On a piece of stage furniture:

'The chair ... was upholstered in one of those flagrant chintzes, designed, apparently, by the art editor of a seed catalogue.'

Frank Lloyd Wright
On television:

'Chewing gum for the eyes.'

William Wycherley
'Next to the pleasure of making a new mistress is that of being rid of an old one.'

Israel Zangwill
On fellow writer George Bernard Shaw:

'The way Bernard Shaw believes in himself is very refreshing in these atheistic days when so many people believe in no God at all.'

A few anonymous flashes
At the formal empanelling at the start of the day's proceedings one of the jurymen asked the judge:

'My lord, I hope I may be exempted from service today – my wife is expecting a conception.'

'I think you mean a confinement,' his lordship replied, 'but whatever it is I agree that you should be there.'

The visiting preacher had a word with the vicar in the vestry before they went to greet the congregation at the church door.

'I hope that I didn't weary them by the length of my sermon.'

'No, indeed, nor by its depth,' said his colleague.

'Is this pig?' asked the ill-mannered guest holding up a

piece of meat on his fork, in the mistaken belief that he was witty.

'To which end of the fork do you refer?' asked the guest who was.

Halfway through an hour-long lecture one of the students, bored by what was evidently way above his head, stood up and walked out of the lecture hall.

'Young man,' the lecturer called after him. 'Come back, you seem to have forgotten something.'

'What?' said the student.

'Your manners,' the lecturer replied.

The famous nineteenth-century tragic actress, Rachel, was talking in the wings about the evening's performance:

'*Mon dieu!* When I came out on stage the audience simply sat there open-mouthed.'

'Rubbish!' said one of the younger members of the cast. 'They never all yawn at once.'

'How frequently do aircraft of this type crash?' one of the more tedious passengers asked an air hostess as they were fastening their seat-belts for take-off.

'Only once,' she told him.

Not long after all guests had been seated at an embassy dinner one of the female guests complained that, according to the strict order of precedence, she should have been sitting next to the ambassador and not halfway down the table as was the case. After several whispered enquires she was proved right and the whole line of guests had to move down one seat to make room for her. Once she was settled into her rightful seat she turned to her host to apologise for the disturbance which she had caused.

'I expect you and your wife must find these questions of protocol extremely troublesome, your Excellency?'

'Not really' the ambassador replied. 'We have found by experience that those people who matter don't mind and those who mind don't matter.'

'I've come to my wit's end,' he told his friend.

'Well, you can't have had far to travel,' came the comforting reply.

'You are very aggressive, my dear,' the vicar said to his rebellious daughter. 'Do remember what St. Matthew tells us about the meek inheriting the earth.'

'I'm sure they will, Daddy,' she said, 'when the others have finished with it.'

Shortly after the beginning of the second act, the critic got up from his seat to leave the theatre.

'Don't go yet,' urged the producer. 'I promise you there's a terrific kick in the next scene.'

'Keep it for the author,' said the critic, and left.

'I intend to speak on the subject of "The Milk of Human Kindness",' the habitually long-winded preacher told the vicar whose parish he was visiting.

'Indeed,' said the vicar. 'Condensed I hope.'

Exasperated director to violently energetic, young actress:

'Darling, if only you threw your voice about as much as you do your body, we might get somewhere.'

As the millionaire's wife descended from her limousine, holding her poodle with a jewelled collar, and made her way towards the door of the restaurant, a dishevelled old woman, with newspapers tied round her legs, dragging a plastic sack behind,

hobbled up to her saying:

'Please help me, madam, I haven't eaten for three days.'

'Well, my dear,' the rich lady told her, 'you must simply force yourself.'

The Last Word

Essentially, sarcasm is about having the last word. In the wicked world of wounding wit, there's nothing more frustrating (or humiliating) than playing what you fondly believed was an unbeatable ace only to find yourself trumped.

Unfortunately, there's only one moment in our lives when we can be sure of getting the last word – and that's on our deathbed. In every other situation, our victims have a chance to match our sarcasm with their own or, worse still, to get their own back by other means: the traffic warden may be smarting beneath the whiplash of your caustic wit, but he can still slap on that £6 ticket; the bank manager may blanch in the face of your withering scorn, but he can still refuse the overdraft; your neighbours may recoil nervously at the cutting edge of your sarcastic sophistry, but they can still turn the stereo up louder than ever. However, nobody, but nobody, can get back at you once you've spoken your last.

As someone who is used to living fairly close to death (my house backs on to a cemetery) it occurred to me that it might be appropriate for the last words in a book about the art (and craft) of delivering last words to the living, to be some of the Famous Last Words of the dead.

They're not all sarcastic (or sad, for that matter), but they are all memorable lines that definitely allowed their utterers the ultimate last word.

* * *

Agrippina (1559 AD), mother of the Emperor Nero. To the assassins sent by her son:
'Smite my womb.'

Alexander the Great (356–323 BC) asked who was to succeed him:
'The strongest.'

Ethan Allan (1738–89), officer during the American Revolution. On being told that the angels were waiting for him:
'Waiting are they? Waiting are they? Well, let 'em wait!'

Albert Anastasia (d. 1957), gangster. On being shot while in a barber's chair:
'Haircut!'

John Barrymore (1882–1942), actor. To his old friend Gene Fowler:
'Tell me, Gene, is it true that you're the illegitimate son of Buffalo Bill?'

Henry Ward Beecher (1813–87), Congregationalist preacher:
'Now comes the mystery.'

Ludwig van Beethoven (1770–1827)
'Friends applaud, the Comedy is over.'

Alexander Graham Bell (1847–1922). When asked not to hurry his dictation:
'But I have to. So little done. So much to do!'

Ryumin Michael Bestuzhev (d. 1826), Russian revolutionary. After the first rope had broken:

'Nothing succeeds with me. Even here I meet with disappointment.'

Dominique Bouhors (d. 1702), French grammarian:
'I am about to, or, I am going to die. Either expression is used.'

Andrew Bradford (d. 1742), publisher of the first newspaper in Philadelphia:
'Oh Lord, forgive the errata!'

John Philpot Curran (1750–1817), Irish writer and orator. To his doctor, who told him he was coughing with 'more difficulty':
'That is surprising, since I have been practising all night.'

Diogenes the Cynic (412–323 BC), Greek philosopher.

Xeniades:	'How do you want to be buried?'
Diogenes:	'Face downwards.'
Xeniades:	'Why?'
Diogenes:	'Because everything will shortly be turned upside down.'

Anthony J. Drexell III (d. 1893), socialite. Demonstrating a new pistol, he accidentally shot himself:
'Here's one you've never seen before. . . .'

Frederick William I (1688–1740), King of Prussia. Hearing the passage from the Book of Job, 'Naked I came into the world and naked shall go', he answered:
'No, not quite naked; I shall have my uniform on.'

Thomas Gainsborough (1727–88), English painter:

'We are all going to Heaven and Van Dyck is of the company.'

Heinrich Heine (1797–1856), German poet. Asked if he was at peace with God:
'Do not trouble yourself. God will pardon me: it's His profession.'

Abram S. Hewitt (1822–1903), industrialist. Removing his oxgyen tube from his mouth:
'And now I am officially dead.'

Terry Kath (d. 1978), rock musician. Playing Russian roulette with a loaded revolver:
'Don't worry, it's not loaded.'

Ronald Knox (1888–1957), English theologian and essayist. Asked if he would like to hear an extract from his own version of the Bible, he declined:
'Awfully jolly of you to suggest it, though.'

Karl Marx (1818–83). To his housekeeper who asked whether he had a final message for the world:
'Go on, get out! Last words are for fools who haven't said enough.'

W. Somerset Maugham (1874–1965)
'Dying is a very dull, dreary affair. And my advice to you is to have nothing whatever to do with it.'

Thomas Paine (1737–1809), radical political theorist, born in England, died in America:
His doctor: 'Your belly diminished.'
Paine: 'And yours augments.'

Viscount Henry John Temple Palmerston (1784–1865)

'Die, my dear doctor? That's the last thing I shall do.'

James W. Rodgers (1911–60), murderer, executed by a firing squad in Utah. Asked whether he had a final request:
    'Why, yes – a bullet-proof vest.'

Robbie Ross (d. 1918), friend of Oscar Wilde. Punning on Keat's epitaph:
    'Here lies one whose name was written in hot water.'

John Sedgwick (1813–64), American Civil War general. Peering over the parapet at the battle of Spotsylvania:
    'They couldn't hit an elephant at this dist . . .'

Sir Ernest Henry Shackleton (1874–1922), explorer. To his doctor:
    'You are always wanting me to give up something. What do you want me to give up now?'

Lytton Strachey (1880–1938), English biographer and critic:
    'If this is dying, I don't think much of it.'

Tamburlaine (1336–1405), Mongol leader:
    'Never has death been frightened away by screaming.'

Oscar Wilde (1856–1900). Calling for champagne:
    'I am dying, as I have lived, beyond my means.'

If you've got this far and you've come to the conclusion that, while there are times when you envy the great masters of sarcastic wit, on the whole you'd rather be you and alive than dead and Oscar Wilde, I think you're right. And what's more you don't have to worry about it – because, come what may, you can still come out on top. When you're next faced with a situation that cries out for a caustic comment, don't do a thing. When you're next confronted with a provocative volley of scorn don't say a word. Instead, remember what G.K. Chesterton once said: 'Silence is the unbearable repartee.'

YOU'LL BE ASTONISHED BY

What *This* Katie Did

the dramatic real-life story of

Katie Boyle

Katie Boyle is known to millions as the charming and glamorous TV personality. Her image is that of someone cool, calm and collected – and above all – terribly proper. But appearances can be deceptive . . .

Born Caterina Irene Elena Maria Imperiali de Francavilla, the daughter of an eccentric Italian marquis, Katie Boyle's life has been *far* from uneventful. Expelled from four out of her six schools, imprisoned in her father's villa as a teenager, she escaped to join her Italian lover (who was later shot by the partisans). Her father recaptured her and she was incarcerated in a lunatic asylum for a year until she was rescued by her mother and brought to England.

WHAT *THIS* KATIE DID is the fascinating and often startling account of Katie Boyle's childhood, her loves, her three marriages and her successful TV career. Above all, it is the remarkable story of the delightful woman who is Katie Boyle.

AUTOBIOGRAPHY   0 7221 1787 6   £1.75

MEN
EXASPERATING TO LIVE WITH.
IMPOSSIBLE TO LIVE WITHOUT.

The Classified MAN

TWENTY-TWO TYPES OF MEN
(and what to do about them)

Susanna M. Hoffman

Look out for:—

The Instant Barricader – he comes on like a hurricane and disappears just as fast.

The Idle Lord – he believes that money was made to be spent – *yours* on *him*.

The Man Who Would Be Mogul – he lives solely for business. All other things – women, children, friends, holocausts, funerals – come second.

Recognise somebody? If not, you'll certainly find him between the covers of Ms. Hoffman's hilarious book. A book that no women should be without.

GENERAL   0 7221 4603 5   £1.50

THE ELDORADO NETWORK

BY DEREK ROBINSON

1941. Hitler rampant. Spain neutral. Madrid the
launching-pad for spies from each side.
One of the most audacious of these spies was codenamed
'Eldorado'. He had no right to survive, let alone succeed –
he was far too young, inexperienced, and impetuous.
Nevertheless he prospered and set up a network of agents
whose information proved so valuable that it altered the
course of the war. In the process, Eldorado made a lot of
money. He also made a lot of very dangerous enemies.
Soon the big question was: who would hit the target first?
Would Eldorado turn himself into a millionaire before his
enemies could turn him into a corpse?

THE ELDORADO NETWORK was inspired by the known
facts about the daring and outrageous career of the 'Eldorado'
who really existed.

'Spy thrillers usually leave me cold, but this one is plainly
outstanding in its class'
GUARDIAN

FICTION/WAR   0 7221 7421 7   £1.50

And don't miss
KRAMER'S WAR
by Derek Robinson, also available in Sphere Books

A selection of bestsellers from SPHERE

FICTION

CHAMELEON	William Diehl	£2.25 ☐
THE CAMBODIA FILE	J. Anderson &	
	B. Pronzini	£2.25 ☐
TRANCE	Derek Lambert	£1.75 ☐
THE STONE FLOWER	Alan Scholefield	£1.95 ☐
TWIN CONNECTIONS	Justine Valenti	£1.75 ☐

FILM & TV TIE-INS

E.T. THE EXTRA-TERRESTRIAL	William Kotzwinkle	£1.50 ☐
THE IRISH R.M.	E. E. Somerville & M. Ross	£1.95 ☐
THE GENTLE TOUCH	Terence Feely	£1.50 ☐
THE PROFESSIONALS:		
OPERATION SUSIE &	Ken Blake	£1.25 ☐
YOU'LL BE ALL RIGHT	Ken Blake	£1.25 ☐

NON-FICTION

THE NUCLEAR BARONS	P. Pringle & J. Spigelman	£3.50 ☐
THE HEALTH & FITNESS		
HANDBOOK	Ed. Miriam Polunin	£5.95 ☐
NELLA LAST'S WAR	Nella Last	£1.95 ☐
ONE CHILD	Torey L. Hayden	£1.75 ☐

All Sphere books are available at your local bookshop or newsagent, or can be ordered direct from the publisher. Just tick the titles you want and fill in the form below.

Name _____

Address _____

_____

Write to Sphere Books, Cash Sales Department, P.O. Box 11, Falmouth, Cornwall TR10 9EN

Please enclose a cheque or postal order to the value of the cover price plus:

UK: 45p for the first book, 20p for the second book and 14p for each additional book ordered to a maximum charge of £1.63.

OVERSEAS: 75p for the first book plus 21p per copy for each additional book.

BFPO & EIRE: 45p for the first book, 20p for the second book plus 14p per copy for the next 7 books, thereafter 8p per book.

Sphere Books reserve the right to show new retail prices on covers which may differ from those previously advertised in the text or elsewhere, and to increase postal rates in accordance with the PO.